May 2009

PENGUIN BOOKS — GREAT IDEAS

On the Suffering of the World

Arthur Schopenhauer
1788–1860

Arthur Schopenhauer

On the Suffering of the World

TRANSLATED BY R. J. HOLLINGDALE

PENGUIN BOOKS — GREAT IDEAS

PENGUIN BOOKS

Published by the Penguin Group
Penguin Books Ltd, 80 Strand, London WC2R 0RL, England
Penguin Group (USA) Inc., 375 Hudson Street, New York, New York 10014, USA
Penguin Books Australia Ltd, 250 Camberwell Road,
Camberwell, Victoria 3124, Australia
Penguin Books Canada Ltd, 10 Alcorn Avenue, Toronto, Ontario, Canada M4V 3B2
Penguin Books India (P) Ltd, 11 Community Centre,
Panchsheel Park, New Delhi – 110 017, India
Penguin Group (NZ), Cnr Airborne and Rosedale Roads,
Albany, Auckland 1310, New Zealand
Penguin Books (South Africa) (Pty) Ltd, 24 Sturdee Avenue,
Rosebank 2196, South Africa

Penguin Books Ltd, Registered Offices: 80 Strand, London WC2R 0RL, England

www.penguin.com

Parerga and Paralipomena first published 1850
First published in Penguin Classics as *Essays and Aphorisms* 1970
This selection first published in Penguin Books 2004

14

Translation copyright © R. J. Hollingdale, 1970
All rights reserved

Taken from the Penguin Classics edition of *Essays and Aphorisms*, translated and
introduced by R. J. Hollingdale

Set in Monotype Dante
Typeset by Rowland Phototypesetting Ltd, Bury St Edmunds, Suffolk
Printed in England by Clays Ltd, St Ives plc

ISBN-13: 978-0-141-01894-2

www.greenpenguin.co.uk

Mixed Sources
Product group from well-managed
forests and other controlled sources
www.fsc.org Cert no. SA-COC-1592
© 1996 Forest Stewardship Council

Penguin Books is committed to a sustainable future
for our business, our readers and our planet.
The book in your hands is made from paper
certified by the Forest Stewardship Council.

Contents

ESSAYS

On the Suffering of the World

If the immediate and direct purpose of our life is not suffering then our existence is the most ill-adapted to its purpose in the world: for it is absurd to suppose that the endless affliction of which the world is everywhere full, and which arises out of the need and distress pertaining essentially to life, should be purposeless and purely accidental. Each individual misfortune, to be sure, seems an exceptional occurrence; but misfortune in general is the rule.

Just as a stream flows smoothly on as long as it encounters no obstruction, so the nature of man and animal is such that we never really notice or become conscious of what is agreeable to our will; if we are to notice something, our will has to have been thwarted, has to have experienced a shock of some kind. On the other hand, all that opposes, frustrates and resists our will, that is to say all that is unpleasant and painful, impresses itself upon us instantly, directly and with great clarity. Just as we are conscious not of the healthiness of our whole body but only of the little place where the shoe pinches, so we think not of the totality of our successful activities but of some insignificant trifle or other which continues to vex us. On this fact is founded what I have often before drawn attention to: the negativity of well-being and happiness, in antithesis to the positivity of pain.

I therefore know of no greater absurdity than that absurdity which characterizes almost all metaphysical systems: that of explaining evil as something negative. For evil is precisely that which is positive, that which makes itself palpable; and good, on the other hand, i.e. all happiness and all gratification, is that which is negative, the mere abolition of a desire and extinction of a pain.

This is also consistent with the fact that as a rule we find pleasure much less pleasurable, pain much more painful than we expected.

A quick test of the assertion that enjoyment outweighs pain in this world, or that they are at any rate balanced, would be to compare the feelings of an animal engaged in eating another with those of the animal being eaten.

3

The most effective consolation in every misfortune and every affliction is to observe others who are more unfortunate than we: and everyone can do this. But what does that say for the condition of the whole?

History shows us the life of nations and finds nothing to narrate but wars and tumults; the peaceful years appear only as occasional brief pauses and interludes. In just the same way the life of the individual is a constant struggle, and not merely a metaphorical one against want or boredom, but also an actual struggle against other people. He discovers adversaries everywhere, lives in continual conflict and dies with sword in hand.

4

Not the least of the torments which plague our existence is the constant pressure of *time*, which never lets us so much as draw breath but pursues us all like a taskmaster with a whip. It ceases to persecute only him it has delivered over to boredom.

5

And yet, just as our body would burst asunder if the pressure of the atmosphere were removed from it, so would the arrogance of men expand, if not to the point of bursting then to that of the most unbridled folly, indeed madness, if the pressure of want, toil, calamity and frustration were removed from their life. One can even say that we *require* at all times a certain quantity of care or sorrow or want, as a ship requires ballast, in order to keep on a straight course.

Work, worry, toil and trouble are indeed the lot of almost all men their whole life long. And yet if every desire were satisfied as soon as it arose how would men occupy their lives, how would they pass the time? Imagine this race transported to a Utopia where everything grows of its own accord and turkeys fly around ready-roasted, where lovers find one another without any delay and keep one another without any difficulty: in such a place some men would die of boredom or hang themselves, some would fight and kill one another, and thus they would create for themselves more suffering than nature inflicts on them as it is. Thus for a race such as this no stage, no form of existence is suitable other than the one it already possesses.

6

Since, as we recalled above, pleasure and well-being is negative and suffering positive, the happiness of a given life is not to be measured according to the joys and pleasures it contains but according to the absence of the positive element, the absence of suffering. This being so, however, the lot of the animals appears more endurable than that of man. Let us look at both a little more closely.

However varied the forms may be which human happiness and misery assume, inciting man to seek the one and flee from the other, the material basis of them all is physical pleasure or physical pain. This basis is very narrow: it consists of health, food, protection from wet and cold, and sexual gratification; or the lack of these things. Man has, consequently, no larger share of real physical pleasure than the animals have, except perhaps to the extent that his more highly charged nervous system intensifies every sensation of pleasure – as it also does every sensation of pain. Yet how much stronger are the emotions aroused in him than those aroused in the animals! how incomparably more profound and vehement are his passions! – and all to achieve exactly the same result in the end: health, food, covering, etc.

This arises first and foremost because with him everything is powerfully intensified by thinking about absent and future things, and this is in fact the origin of care, fear and hope, which, once they have been aroused, make a far stronger impression on men than do actual present pleasures or sufferings, to which the animal is limited. For, since it lacks the faculty of reflection, joys and sorrows cannot accumulate in the animal as they do in man through memory and anticipation. With the animal, present suffering, even if repeated countless times, remains what it was the first time: it cannot sum itself up. Hence the enviable composure and unconcern which characterizes the animal. With man, on the other hand, there evolves out of those elements of pleasure and suffering which he has in common with the animal an intensification of his sensations of happiness and misery which can lead to momentary transports which may sometimes even prove fatal, or to suicidal despair. More closely considered, what happens is this: he deliberately intensifies his needs, which are originally scarcely harder to satisfy than those of the animal, so as to intensify his pleasure: hence luxury, confectionery, tobacco, opium, alcoholic drinks, finery and all that pertains to them. To these is then added, also as a result of reflection, a source of pleasure, and consequently of suffering, available to him alone and one which preoccupies him beyond all measure, indeed more than all the rest put together: ambition and the sense of honour and shame – in plain words, what he thinks others think of him. This, in a thousand, often curious shapes then becomes the goal of all those endeavours of his which go beyond physical pleasure or pain. He excels the animal in his capacity for enjoying intellectual pleasures, to be sure, and these are available to him in many degrees, from the simplest jesting and conversation up to the highest achievements of the mind; but as a counterweight to this, on the side of suffering stands boredom, which is unknown to the animals at least in the state of nature and is only very slightly perceptible in the very cleverest domesticated ones, while to man it has become a veritable scourge. Want and boredom are indeed the twin poles of human life. Finally it remains to be mentioned that with man sexual gratification is tied to a very obstinate selectivity which is sometimes intensified into a more or less passionate love. Thus sexuality becomes for man a source of brief pleasure and protracted suffering.

It is indeed remarkable how, through the mere addition of thought, which the animal lacks, there should have been erected on the same narrow basis of pain and pleasure that the animal possesses so vast and lofty a structure of human happiness and misery, and man should be subjected to such vehement emotions, passions and convulsions that their impress can be read in enduring lines on his face; while all the time and in reality he is concerned only with the very same things which the animal too attains, and attains with an incomparably smaller expenditure of emotion. Through all this, however, the measure of suffering increases in man far more than the enjoyment, and it is very greatly enhanced specifically by the fact that he actually *knows* of death, while the animal only instinctively flees it without actually knowing of it and therefore without ever really having it in view, which man does all the time.

The animals are much more content with mere existence than we are; the plants are wholly so; and man is so according to how dull and insensitive he is. The animal's life consequently contains less suffering but also less pleasure than the human's, the direct reason being that on the one hand it is free from care and anxiety and the torments that attend them, but on the other is without hope and therefore has no share in that anticipation of a happy future which, together with the enchanting products of the imagination which accompany it, is the source of most of our greatest joys and pleasures. The animal lacks both anxiety and hope because its consciousness is restricted to what is clearly evident and thus to the present moment: the animal is the present incarnate. But precisely because this is so it appears in one respect to be truly sagacious compared with us, namely in its peaceful, untroubled enjoyment of the present: its obvious composure often puts to shame our own frequently restless and discontented condition.

7

If the above discussion has demonstrated that the reason man's life is more full of suffering than the animal's is his greater capacity for knowledge, we can now trace this back to a more general law and thus attain to a much more comprehensive view.

Knowledge is in itself always painless. Pain affects only the will and consists in an obstruction, impediment or frustration of it: nonetheless, this frustration of the will, if it is to be felt as pain, must be accompanied by knowledge. That is why even physical pain is conditioned by the nerves and their connexion with the brain, so that an injury to a limb is not felt if the nerves leading from the limb to the brain are severed or the brain itself is devitalized by chloroform. That spiritual pain is conditional upon knowledge goes without saying, and it is easy to see that it will increase with the degree of knowledge. We can thus express the whole relationship figuratively by saying that the will is the string, its frustration or impediment the vibration of the string, knowledge the sounding-board, and pain the sound.

Now this means that not only inorganic matter but the plant too is incapable of feeling pain, however many frustrations its will may undergo. On the other hand, every animal, even an *infusorium*, suffers pain, because knowledge, however imperfect, is the true characteristic of animality. At each higher stage of animal life there is a corresponding increase in pain. In the lowest animals it is extremely slight, but even in the highest it nowhere approaches the pain which man is capable of feeling, since even the highest animals lack thought and concepts. And it is right that this capacity for pain should reach its zenith only where, by virtue of the existence of reason, there also exists the possibility of denial of the will: for otherwise it would be nothing but aimless cruelty.

8

In our early youth we sit before the life that lies ahead of us like children sitting before the curtain in a theatre, in happy and tense anticipation of whatever is going to appear. Luckily we do not know what really will appear. For to him who does know, children can sometimes seem like innocent delinquents, sentenced not to death but to life, who have not yet discovered what their punishment will consist of. Nonetheless, everyone desires to achieve old age, that is to say a condition in which one can say: 'Today it is bad, and day by day it will get worse – until at last the worst of all arrives.'

9

If you imagine, in so far as it is approximately possible, the sum total of distress, pain and suffering of every kind which the sun shines upon in its course, you will have to admit it would have been much better if the sun had been able to call up the phenomenon of life as little on the earth as on the moon; and if, here as there, the surface were still in a crystalline condition.

You can also look upon our life as an episode unprofitably disturbing the blessed calm of nothingness. In any case, even he who has found life tolerably bearable will, the longer he lives, feel the more clearly that on the whole it is a disappointment, nay a cheat.* If two men who were friends in youth meet in old age after the lapse of an entire generation, the principal feeling the sight of one another, linked as it is with recollections of earlier years, will arouse in both will be one of total disappointment with the whole of life, which once lay so fair before them in the rosy dawn of youth, promised so much and performed so little. This feeling will dominate so decidedly over every other that they will not even think it necessary to speak of it but will silently assume it as the basis of their conversation.

If the act of procreation were neither the outcome of

---

* The last four words are in English in the original.

a desire nor accompanied by feelings of pleasure, but a matter to be decided on the basis of purely rational considerations, is it likely the human race would still exist? Would each of us not rather have felt so much pity for the coming generation as to prefer to spare it the burden of existence, or at least not wish to take it upon himself to impose that burden upon it in cold blood?

For the world is Hell, and men are on the one hand the tormented souls and on the other the devils in it.

Brahma is supposed to have created the world by a kind of fall into sin, or by an error, and has to atone for this sin or error by remaining in it himself until he has redeemed himself out of it. Very good! In *Buddhism* the world arises as a consequence of an inexplicable clouding of the heavenly clarity of the blessed state of Nirvana after a long period of quietude. Its origin is thus a kind of fatality which is fundamentally to be understood in a moral sense, notwithstanding the case has an exact analogy in the physical world in the origin of the sun in an inexplicable primeval streak of mist. Subsequently, however, as a consequence of moral misdeeds it gradually deteriorates physically too, until it has assumed its present sad condition. Excellent! To the *Greeks* the world and the gods were the work of an unfathomable necessity: that will do as a provisional explanation. *Ormuzd* is continually at war with *Ahriman*: that is worth considering.* But that a god like *Jehovah* should create this world

* Brahma is the principal deity of Hinduism. Ormuzd is the good God, Ahriman the bad God of Zoroastrianism, the ancient religion of Persia.

of want and misery *animi causa** and *de gaieté de cœur* and then go so far as to applaud himself for it, saying it is all very good: that is quite unacceptable.

Even if Leibniz's demonstration that this is the best of all *possible* worlds were correct, it would still not be a vindication of divine providence. For the Creator created not only the world, he also created possibility itself: therefore he should have created the possibility of a better world than this one.

In general, however, two things cry out against any such view of the world as the successful work of an infinitely wise, infinitely good and at the same time infinitely powerful being: the misery of which it is full and the obvious imperfection of its most highly developed phenomenon, man, who is indeed a grotesque caricature. This is a dissonance that cannot be resolved. On the contrary, it is precisely these instances which support what we have been saying and which provide evidence for our conception of the world as the product of our own sins and therefore as something that had better not have been. Under the former conception they become a bitter indictment of the Creator and supply material for cynicisms, while under our conception they appear as an indictment of our own nature and will, and one calculated to teach us humility. For they lead us to the insight that, like the children of libertine fathers, we come into the world already encumbered with guilt and that it is only because we have continually to atone for this guilt that our existence is so wretched and its end

* Capriciously, voluntarily.

is death. Nothing is more certain than that, generally speaking, it is the grievous *sin of the world* which gives rise to the manifold and great *suffering of the world*; whereby is meant not any physical-empirical connexion but a metaphysical one. The story of the Fall is consequently the only thing which reconciles me to the Old Testament; I even regard it as the sole metaphysical truth contained in that book, even though it does appear clothed in allegory. For our existence resembles nothing so much as the consequence of a misdeed, punishment for a forbidden desire.

As a reliable compass for orientating yourself in life nothing is more useful than to accustom yourself to regarding this world as a place of atonement, a sort of penal colony. When you have done this you will order your expectations of life according to the nature of things and no longer regard the calamities, sufferings, torments and miseries of life as something irregular and not to be expected but will find them entirely in order, well knowing that each of us is here being punished for his existence and each in his own particular way. This outlook will enable us to view the so-called imperfections of the majority of men, i.e. their moral and intellectual shortcomings and the facial appearance resulting therefrom, without surprise and certainly without indignation: for we shall always bear in mind where we are and consequently regard every man first and foremost as a being who exists only as a consequence of his culpability and whose life is an expiation of the crime of being born.

The conviction that the world, and therefore man too,

is something which really ought not to exist is in fact calculated to instil in us indulgence towards one another: for what can be expected of beings placed in such a situation as we are? From this point of view one might indeed consider that the appropriate form of address between man and man ought to be, not *monsieur, sir*, but *fellow sufferer, compagnon de misères*. However strange this may sound it corresponds to the nature of the case, makes us see other men in a true light and reminds us of what are the most necessary of all things: tolerance, patience, forbearance and charity, which each of us needs and which each of us therefore owes.

On the Vanity of Existence

The vanity of existence is revealed in the whole form existence assumes: in the infiniteness of time and space contrasted with the finiteness of the individual in both; in the fleeting present as the sole form in which actuality exists; in the contingency and relativity of all things; in continual becoming without being; in continual desire without satisfaction; in the continual frustration of striving of which life consists. *Time* and that *perishability* of all things existing in time that time itself brings about is simply the form under which the will to live, which as thing in itself is imperishable, reveals to itself the vanity of its striving. Time is that by virtue of which everything becomes nothingness in our hands and loses all real value.

That which *has been* no longer *is*; it as little exists as does that which has *never* been. But everything that *is* in the next moment *has been*. Thus the most insignificant present has over the most significant past the advantage of *actuality*, which means that the former bears to the latter the relation of something to nothing.

To our amazement we suddenly exist, after having

for countless millennia not existed; in a short while we will again not exist, also for countless millennia. That cannot be right, says the heart: and even upon the crudest intelligence there must, when it considers such an idea, dawn a presentiment of the ideality of time. This however, together with that of space, is the key to all true metaphysics, because it makes room for a quite different order of things than that of nature. That is why Kant is so great.

Every moment of our life belongs to the present only for a moment; then it belongs for ever to the past. Every evening we are poorer by a day. We would perhaps grow frantic at the sight of this ebbing away of our short span of time were we not secretly conscious in the profoundest depths of our being that we share in the inexhaustible well of eternity, out of which we can for ever draw new life and renewed time.

You could, to be sure, base on considerations of this kind a theory that the greatest *wisdom* consists in enjoying the present and making this enjoyment the goal of life, because the present is all that is real and everything else merely imaginary. But you could just as well call this mode of life the greatest *folly*: for that which in a moment ceases to exist, which vanishes as completely as a dream, cannot be worth any serious effort.

3

Our existence has no foundation on which to rest except the transient present. Thus its form is essentially unceasing *motion*, without any possibility of that repose which we continually strive after. It resembles the course of a man running down a mountain who would fall over if he tried to stop and can stay on his feet only by running on; or a pole balanced on the tip of the finger; or a planet which would fall into its sun if it ever ceased to plunge irresistibly forward. Thus existence is typified by unrest.

In such a world, where no stability of any kind, no enduring state is possible, where everything is involved in restless change and confusion and keeps itself on its tightrope only by continually striding forward – in such a world, happiness is not so much as to be thought of. It cannot dwell where nothing occurs but Plato's 'continual becoming and never being'. In the first place, no man is happy but strives his whole life long after a supposed happiness which he seldom attains, and even if he does it is only to be disappointed with it; as a rule, however, he finally enters harbour shipwrecked and dismasted. In the second place, however, it is all one whether he has been happy or not in a life which has consisted merely of a succession of transient present moments and is now at an end.

4

The scenes of our life resemble pictures in rough mosaic; they are ineffective from close up, and have to be viewed from a distance if they are to seem beautiful. That is why to attain something desired is to discover how vain it is; and why, though we live all our lives in expectation of better things, we often at the same time long regretfully for what is past. The present, on the other hand, is regarded as something quite temporary and serving only as the road to our goal. That is why most men discover when they look back on their life that they have the whole time been living *ad interim*, and are surprised to see that which they let go by so unregarded and unenjoyed was precisely their life, was precisely that in expectation of which they lived.

5

Life presents itself first and foremost as a task: the task of maintaining itself, *de gagner sa vie*.* If this task is accomplished, what has been gained is a burden, and there then appears a second task: that of doing something with it so as to ward off boredom, which hovers over every secure life like a bird of prey. Thus the first task is to gain something and the second to become unconscious of what has been gained, which is otherwise a burden.

That human life must be some kind of mistake is sufficiently proved by the simple observation that man is a compound of needs which are hard to satisfy; that their satisfaction achieves nothing but a painless condition in which he is only given over to boredom; and that boredom is a direct proof that existence is in itself valueless, for boredom is nothing other than the sensation of the emptiness of existence. For if life, in the desire for which our essence and existence consists, possessed in itself a positive value and real content, there would be no such thing as boredom: mere existence would fulfil and satisfy us. As things are, we take no pleasure in existence except when we are striving after

* Of earning one's living.

19

something – in which case distance and difficulties make our goal look as if it would satisfy us (an illusion which fades when we reach it) – or when engaged in purely intellectual activity, in which case we are really stepping out of life so as to regard it from outside, like spectators at a play. Even sensual pleasure itself consists in a continual striving and ceases as soon as its goal is reached. Whenever we are not involved in one or other of these things but directed back to existence itself we are overtaken by its worthlessness and vanity and this is the sensation called boredom.

6

That the most perfect manifestation of the will to live represented by the human organism, with its incomparably ingenious and complicated machinery, must crumble to dust and its whole essence and all its striving be palpably given over at last to annihilation – this is nature's unambiguous declaration that all the striving of this will is essentially vain. If it were something possessing value in itself, something which ought unconditionally to exist, it would not have non-being as its goal.

Yet what a difference there is between our beginning and our end! We begin in the madness of carnal desire and the transport of voluptuousness, we end in the dissolution of all our parts and the musty stench of corpses. And the road from the one to the other too goes, in regard to our well-being and enjoyment of life, steadily downhill: happily dreaming childhood, exultant youth, toil-filled years of manhood, infirm and often wretched old age, the torment of the last illness and finally the throes of death – does it not look as if existence were an error the consequences of which gradually grow more and more manifest?

We shall do best to think of life as a *desengaño*, as a process of disillusionment: since this is, clearly enough, what everything that happens to us is calculated to produce.

On the Antithesis of Thing in Itself and Appearance

Thing in itself signifies that which exists independently of our perception, that which actually is. To Democritus it was matter; fundamentally this is what it still was to Locke; to Kant it was = x; to me it is *will*.*

2

Just as we know of the earth only the surface, not the great, solid masses of the interior, so we know empirically of things and the world nothing at all except their *appearances*, i.e. the surface. Exact knowledge of this constitutes *physics*, taken in the widest sense. But that this surface presupposes an interior which is not merely superficies but possesses cubic content is, together with deductions as to the character of this interior, the theme of *metaphysics*. To seek to construe the nature of things in themselves according to the laws of appearance is an undertaking to be compared with seeking to construe stereometric bodies out of superficies and the laws that apply to them. Every *dogmatic transcendental* philosophy is an attempt to construe the *thing in itself* according to

---

*Democritus (*fl. c.* 420 BC), Greek philosopher, the founder of atomism. John Locke (1632–1704), the representative British philosopher of the late seventeenth century.

the laws of *appearance*, which is like trying to make two absolutely dissimilar bodies cover one another, an attempt which always fails because however you may turn them this or that corner always protrudes.

3

Because everything in nature is at once *appearance* and *thing in itself*, or *natura naturata* and *natura naturans*, it is consequently susceptible of a twofold explanation, a *physical* and a *metaphysical*. The physical explanation is always in terms of *cause*, the metaphysical in terms of *will*; for that which appears in cognitionless nature as *natural force*, and on a higher level as *life force*, receives in animal and man the name *will*. Strictly speaking, therefore, the degree and tendency of a man's intelligence and the constitution of his moral character could perhaps be traced back to purely *physical* causes, the former from the constitution of his brain and nervous system, together with the blood circulation which affects them, the latter from the constitution and combined effect of his heart, vascular system, blood, lungs, liver, spleen, kidneys, intestines, genitalia, etc.; which would, I grant, demand a much more exact knowledge of the laws governing the *rapport du physique au moral** than even Bichat and Cabanis possessed.† Both could then be further traced back to their more remote physical cause, namely the constitution of his parents, inasmuch as these

---

* Relationship between the physical and the moral.

† Marie François Xavier Bichat (1771–1802), anatomist and physiologist. Pierre Jean Georges Cabanis (1757–1808), physician and writer on medicine.

could furnish the seed only for a similar being and not for one higher or better. *Metaphysically*, on the other hand, the same man would have to be explained as the apparitional form of his own, utterly free and primal will, which has created for itself the intellect appropriate to it; so that all his actions, however necessarily they may be the result of his character in conflict with the motivations acting on him at any given time, and however necessarily these again may arise as a consequence of his corporeity, are nonetheless to be attributed wholly to him.

4

When we perceive and consider the existence, life and activity of any natural creature, e.g. an animal, it stands before us, everything zoology and zootomy teaches notwithstanding, as an unfathomable mystery. But must nature then, from sheer obduracy, for ever remain dumb to our questioning? Is nature not, as everything great is, open, communicative and even naïve? Can her failure to reply ever be for any other reason than that we have asked the wrong question, that our question has been based on false presuppositions, that it has even harboured a contradiction? For can it be imagined that a connexion between causes and consequences could exist in nature which is essentially and for ever undiscoverable? – No, certainly not. Nature is unfathomable because we seek after causes and consequences in a realm where this form is not to be found. We try to reach the inner being of nature, which looks out at us from every phenomenon, under the guidance of the principle of sufficient reason

– whereas this is merely the form under which our intellect comprehends appearance, i.e. the surface of things, while we want to employ it beyond the bounds of appearance; for within these bounds it is serviceable and sufficient. Here, for example, the existence of a given animal can be explained by its procreation. This is fundamentally no more mysterious than the issuing of any other effect, even the simplest, from its cause, inasmuch as even in the simplest case the explanation finally strikes the incomprehensible. That in the case of procreation we lack a couple more stages in the causal connexion makes no essential difference, for even if we had them we should still stand at last before the incomprehensible, because appearance remains appearance and does not become thing in itself.

5

We complain of the darkness in which we live out our lives: we do not understand the nature of existence in general; we especially do not know the relation of our own self to the rest of existence. Not only is our life short, our knowledge is limited entirely to it, since we can see neither back before our birth nor out beyond our death, so that our consciousness is as it were a lightning-flash momentarily illuminating the night: it truly seems as though a demon had maliciously shut off all further knowledge from us so as to enjoy our discomfiture.

But this complaint is not really justified: for it arises out of an illusion produced by the false premise that the totality of things proceeded from an *intellect* and consequently existed as an *idea* before it became actual; according to which premise the totality of things, having arisen from the realm of knowledge, must be entirely accessible to knowledge and entirely explicable and capable of being exhaustively comprehended by it. – But the truth of the matter is, I fear, that all that of which we complain of not knowing is not known to anyone, indeed is probably as such unknowable, i.e. not capable of being conceived.* For the *idea*, in whose domain all knowledge lies and to which all knowledge therefore refers, is only the outer side of existence, something secondary, supplementary, something, that is, which was necessary not for the preservation of things as such, the universal totality, but merely for the preservation of the individual animal being. Consequently the existence of things as a whole entered into the realm of knowledge only *per accidens*,† thus to a very limited extent: it forms only the background of the painting in the animal consciousness, where the objectives of the will are the essential element and occupy the front rank. There then arose through this *accidens* the entire world of space and time, i.e. the world as idea, which possesses no existence of this sort at all outside the realm of knowledge. Now since knowledge exists only for the purpose of preserving each animal individual, its whole constitution, all its forms, such as time, space, etc., are adapted merely to the aims of such an individual: and these require

* *Nicht vorstellbar*: not imaginable or conceivable; but in Schopenhauer's usage also bearing the more specific sense of 'not able to be a *Vorstellung*, an *idea*'.
† Accidentally.

knowledge only of relations between individual phenomena and by no means knowledge of the essential nature
of things and the universal totality.

Kant has demonstrated that the problems of metaphysics which trouble everyone to a greater or less
degree are capable of no direct solution and of no satisfac-
tory solution at all. The reason for this is ultimately that
they have their origin in the forms of our intellect – time,
space and causality – while this intellect is designed
merely to prescribe to the individual will its motivations,
i.e. to indicate to it the objectives of its desires, together
with the means of taking possession of them. But if this
intellect is abused by being directed upon the being in
itself of things, upon the totality and the inner constitution of the world, then the aforesaid forms of the
contiguity, successiveness and interdependence of all
possible things give birth to metaphysical problems such
as those of the origin and purpose, the beginning and
end of the world and of one's own self, of the annihilation
of this through death or its continued existence in spite
of death, of freedom of will, and so forth. If we imagine
these forms for once removed, however, and a consciousness of things nonetheless still present, then these
problems would be, not solved, but non-existent: they
would utterly vanish, and the sentences expressing them
would no longer have any meaning. For they arise entirely out of these forms, whose object is not an understanding of the world and existence, but merely an
understanding of our own aims.

This whole way of looking at the question offers us
an explanation and *objective* proof of the Kantian theory,

which its originator proved only from the *subjective* point of view, that the forms of reason can be employed only immanently, not transcendentally. For instead of putting it in this manner one could say: the intellect is physical not metaphysical, i.e. since, as appertaining to the will's objectivization it originates in the will, it exists only to serve the will: this service, however, concerns only things *in* nature, and not things lying outside and beyond nature. It is obvious that an animal possesses intellect only for the purpose of discovering and capturing its food; the degree of intellect it possesses is determined by this purpose. It is no different in the case of man; except that here the greater difficulty of preserving and maintaining him and the endless augmentability of his needs has made necessary a much greater degree of intellect. Only when this is exceeded through an abnormality does there appear a *superfluity of intellect exempt from service*: when this superfluity becomes considerable it is called *genius*. Such an intellect will first of all become *objective*, but it can even go on to become to a certain degree metaphysical, or at least strive to become so: for the consequence of its objectivity is that nature itself, the totality of things, now becomes the intellect's subject-matter and problem. In such an intellect nature first begins properly to perceive itself as something which is and yet could *not* be, or could be *other* than it is; whereas in the ordinary, merely normal intellect nature does not clearly perceive itself – just as the miller does not hear his own mill or the perfumer smell his own shop. To the normal intellect nature appears simply as a matter of course: it is caught up in and encompassed by nature.

Only in certain more luminous moments will it perceive nature and it is then almost terrified at the sight: but the feeling soon passes. What such normal heads can achieve in philosophy, even if they crowd together in their thousands, is consequently easy to imagine; but if intellect were metaphysical, in its origin and in its vocation, it could promote philosophy, especially if its forces were united, as well as it can promote every other science.

On Affirmation and Denial of the Will to Live

It is to some extent obvious *a priori* – *vulgo** it goes without saying – that that which at present produces the phenomenon of the world must be capable of not doing so and consequently remaining inactive. Now if the former state constitutes the phenomenon of the volition of life, the latter will constitute the phenomenon of non-volition. And this will be in its essence identical with the *Magnum Sakhepat* of the Vedanta and the Nirvana of the Buddhists.

The denial of the will to live does not in any way imply the annihilation of a substance; it means merely the act of non-volition: that which previously *willed*, *wills* no more. This *will*, as thing in itself, is known to us only in and through the act of *volition*, and we are therefore incapable of saying or of conceiving what it is or does further after it has ceased to perform this act: thus this denial of the will to live is *for us*, who are phenomena of volition, a transition to nothingness.

---

* '*A priori*': a first principle, acquired by the mind independently of the experience of the senses. '*Vulgo*': generally.

2

Between the ethics of the Greeks and those of the Hindus there exists a glaring antithesis. The object of the former (though with Plato excepted) is to make it possible to lead a happy life, a *vitam beatam*,* that of the latter, on the contrary, to liberate and redeem from life altogether, as is directly stated in the very first sentence of the *Sankhya Karika*.

You perceive a similar contrast – a contrast strengthened by its being in visible form – if you regard the beautiful antique sarcophagus in the gallery at Florence on which is depicted in relief the entire ceremonial of a wedding, from the first proposal to the point where Hymen's torch lights the way to the bridal chamber, and then compare it with a *Christian* coffin, draped in black as a sign of mourning and with a crucifix upon it. The antithesis is in the highest degree significant. Both desire to offer consolation in face of death; they do so in opposite ways, and both are right. The one expresses *affirmation* of the will to life, through which life is assured for all time, however swiftly its figures and forms may succeed one another. The other, by symbols of suffering and death, expresses *denial* of the will to life and redemption from a world in which death and the Devil reign. Between the spirit of Graeco-Roman paganism and the spirit of Christianity the real antithesis is that of affirmation and denial of the will to live – in which regard

* Blessed life.

Christianity is in the last resort fundamentally in the right.

3

My ethics stands in the same relation to that of all other European philosophers as the New Testament does to the Old, taking this relationship in the ecclesiastical sense. For the Old Testament places man under the dominion of the Law, which Law, however, does not lead to redemption. The New Testament, on the other hand, declares that the Law is insufficient and, indeed, absolves man from obedience to it.* In its place it preaches the kingdom of grace, which one can enter through faith, charity and total denial of self: this, it says, is the road to redemption from evil and from the world: for – every Protestant and Rationalist misrepresentation notwithstanding – the true soul of the New Testament is undoubtedly the spirit of asceticism. This spirit of asceticism is precisely denial of the will to live, and the transition from the Old Testament to the New, from the dominion of the Law to the dominion of faith, from justification by works to redemption through the Intercessor, from the dominion of sin and death to eternal life in Christ, signifies, *sensu proprio*,† the transition from merely moral virtue to denial of the will to live. All philosophical ethics before me cleaves to the spirit of the Old Testament: it posits an absolute moral law (i.e. one which has no foundation and no goal) and consists of

---

* Schopenhauer cites Romans vii and Galatians ii and iii.
† In the strict sense.

moral commandments and prohibitions behind which a dictatorial Jehovah is silently introduced; and this is true however different the forms may be in which this ethical philosophy appears. My ethics, on the contrary, possesses foundation, aim and goal: first and foremost, it demonstrates theoretically the metaphysical foundation of justice and charity, and then indicates the goal to which these, if practised in perfection, must ultimately lead. At the same time it candidly confesses the reprehensible nature of the world and points to the denial of the will as the road to redemption from it. My ethics is thus actually in the spirit of the New Testament, while all the others are in that of the Old and consequently amount, even theoretically, to nothing more than Judaism, which is to say naked, despotic theism. In this sense my doctrine could be called the true Christian philosophy, however paradoxical this may seem to those who refuse to penetrate to the heart of the matter but prefer its superficialities.

4

He who is capable of thinking a little more deeply will soon perceive that human desires cannot begin to be sinful simply at that point at which, in their chance encounters with one another, they occasion harm and evil; but that, if this is what they bring about, they must be originally and in their essence sinful and reprehensible, and the entire will to live itself reprehensible. All the cruelty and torment of which the world is full is in fact merely the necessary result of the totality of the forms under which the will to live is objectified, and thus merely a commentary on the affirmation of the will to live. That our existence itself implies guilt is proved by the fact of death.

5

If in comprehending the world you start from the thing in itself, from the will to live, you discover that its kernel, its point of greatest concentration, is the act of generation. What a contrast, on the other hand, is presented if you start from the world of appearance, the empirical world, the world as idea! Here the act of generation is seen as something completely detached and distinct, of subordinate importance, indeed as something secondary to be veiled and hidden, as a paradoxical anomaly offering plentiful material for humour. It might occur to us, however, that this is only a case of the Devil's concealing his game: for has it not been noticed that sexual desire, especially when concentrated into infatuation through fixation on a particular woman, is the quintessence of this noble world's imposture, since it promises so excessively much and performs so miserably little?

The woman's part in procreation is in a certain sense more innocent than the man's, inasmuch as the man gives to the child *will*, which is the prime sin and thus the source of all wickedness and evil, while the woman gives it *knowledge*, which opens the road to salvation. The act of generation is the node of the universe; it declares: 'The will to live is once more affirmed.' Conception and pregnancy, on the other hand, declare: 'To the will there is once more joined the light of knowledge' –

by means of which it can find its way out of the world again and the possibility of redemption is thus once more opened up.

It is this which explains the notable fact that every woman, while she would be ready to die of shame if surprised in the act of generation, nonetheless carries her pregnancy without a trace of shame and indeed with a kind of pride. The reason is that pregnancy is in a certain sense a cancellation of the guilt incurred by coitus: thus coitus bears all the shame and disgrace of the affair, while pregnancy, which is so intimately associated with it, stays pure and innocent and is indeed to some extent sacred.

Coitus is chiefly an affair of the man, pregnancy entirely that of the woman. The child receives from its father will and character, from its mother intellect. The latter is the redeeming principle, the will the principle of bondage. Coitus is the sign that, despite every increase in illumination through the intellect, the will to live continues to exist in time; the renewed incarnation of the will to live is the sign that the light of knowledge, and that in the highest degree of clarity, the possibility of redemption, has again been joined to this will. The sign of this is pregnancy, which therefore goes about frankly and freely, indeed with pride, while coitus hides itself away like a criminal.

6

Unjust or wicked actions are, in regard to him who performs them, signs of the strength of his affirmation of the will to live, and thus of how far he still is from true salvation, which is denial of this will, and from redemption from the world; they are also signs of how long a schooling in knowledge and suffering he still has to undergo before he can attain it. In regard to him who has to suffer these actions, however, although physically they are an evil, metaphysically they are a good and fundamentally beneficial, since they assist him along the road to his true salvation.

7

WORLD SPIRIT: This then is the task of all your labour and all your suffering: it is for this that you *exist*, as all other things exist.

MAN: But what do I get from existence? If it is full I have only distress, if empty only boredom. How can you offer me so poor a reward for so much labour and so much suffering?

WORLD SPIRIT: And yet it is proportionate to all your toil and all your suffering, and is so precisely on account of its meagreness.

MAN: Indeed! That passes my comprehension.

WORLD SPIRIT: I know it does. – (*Aside*) Should I tell him that the value of life lies precisely in this, that it teaches him not to want it? For this supreme initiation life itself must prepare him.

On the Indestructibility of Our Essential Being by Death

You should read Jean Paul's *Selina* to see how a mind of the first order tries to deal with what he comes to think nonsensical in a false concept which he does not want to relinquish because he has set his heart upon it, although he is continually troubled by absurdities he cannot stomach.* The concept in question is that of the continued individual existence of our entire personal consciousness after death. This struggling and wrestling on the part of Jean Paul shows that ideas of this kind, compounded of true and false concepts, are not, as is generally thought, fruitful errors but rather decidedly harmful ones: for the false antithesis between soul and body and the elevation of the total personality to a thing in itself which must endure for ever makes it impossible to arrive at a true knowledge, deriving from the antithesis

* Johannes Paul Friedrich Richter (1763–1825), known by his pen-name of Jean Paul, was one of the most popular German writers of his age. *Selina*, published posthumously in 1827, is an unsuccessful attempt to think clearly what his religious beliefs actually amount to: Jean Paul decides he cannot accept Christianity, but finds it impossible to surrender a number of beliefs, e.g. the belief in immortality, of which he could never have had any conception except as constituents of the Christian religion he rejects.

between appearance and thing in itself, of the indestructibility of our intrinsic being as something unaffected by time, causality and change; moreover, this false concept cannot even be held on to as a surrogate of truth, because reason continually rebels at the absurdity contained in it and is then obliged also to relinquish the truth amalgamated with it. For truth can in the long run endure only in a pure state: tempered with error, it partakes of the frailty of error.

2

If, in everyday life, you are asked about continued existence after death by one of those people who would like to know everything but refuse to learn anything, the most appropriate and approximately correct reply is: 'After your death you will be what you were before your birth.' For this answer implies that it is preposterous to demand that a species of existence which had a beginning should not have an end; in addition, however, it contains a hint that there may be two kinds of existence and, correspondingly, two kinds of nothingness. You might, however, also reply: 'Whatever you will be after your death – even though it were nothing – will then be just as natural and suitable to you as your individual organic existence is now: thus the most you have to fear is the moment of transition. Indeed, since mature consideration of the matter leads to the conclusion that total non-being would be preferable to such an existence as ours is, the idea of the cessation of our existence, or of a time in which we no longer are, can from a rational point of view trouble us as little as the idea that we had never been. Now since this existence is essentially a personal one, the ending of the personality cannot be regarded as a loss.'

3

If we imagine a creature which surveys, knows and understands everything, then the question whether we exist after death would for that creature probably have no meaning, because outside of our present temporal, individual state of being, existence and cessation would no longer signify anything, but would be concepts indistinguishable from one another; so that neither the concept of destruction nor that of continued existence could be applied to our intrinsic and essential being, the thing in itself, of which we are the phenomenal appearance, since these concepts are borrowed from the realm of time, which is merely the form of phenomena. On the other hand, we can imagine the *indestructibility* of this kernel of our phenomenal appearance only as its *continued existence*, and indeed intrinsically only according to the scheme of the *material world*, as which it remains, with all its changes of form, firmly lodged in time. If, now, this kernel is denied its continued existence, we regard our temporal end as an annihilation, according to the scheme of the *form*, which disappears when the material which bears it is withdrawn. Both ideas are, however, a transference of the forms of the phenomenal world on to the thing in itself. But of an indestructibility which is not a continued existence we can hardly construct even an abstract conception, because we lack every intuition for doing so.

In truth, however, the continual coming into existence of new beings and the annihilation of already existing ones is to be regarded as an illusion produced by a contrivance of two lenses (brain-functions) through which alone we can see anything at all: they are called space and time, and in their interpenetration causality. For everything we perceive under these conditions is merely phenomenon; we do not know what things are like in themselves, i.e. independently of our perception of them. This is the actual kernel of the Kantian philosophy.

4

How can one believe that when a human being *dies* a thing in itself has come *to nothing*? Mankind knows, directly and intuitively, that when this happens it is only a phenomenon coming to an end in time, the form of all phenomena, without the thing in itself being affected thereby. We all feel that we are something other than a being which someone once created out of nothing: from this arises the confidence that, while death may be able to end our life, it cannot end our existence.

5

The more clearly you become conscious of the frailty, vanity and dream-like quality of all things, the more clearly will you also become conscious of the eternity of your own inner being; because it is only in contrast to this that the aforesaid quality of things becomes evident, just as you perceive the speed at which a ship is going only when looking at the motionless shore, not when looking into the ship itself.

6

The *present* has two halves: an *objective* and a *subjective*. The objective half alone has the intuition of *time* as its form and thus streams irresistibly away; the subjective half stands firm and thus is always the same. It is from this that there originates our lively recollection of what is long past and, despite our knowledge of the fleetingness of our existence, the consciousness of our immortality.

Whenever we may live we always stand, with our consciousness, at the central point of time, never at its termini, and we may deduce from that that each of us bears within him the unmoving mid-point of the whole of endless time. It is fundamentally this which gives us the confidence to live without being in continual dread of death.

He who, by virtue of the strength of his memory and imagination, can most clearly call up what is long past in his own life will be more conscious than others of the *identity of all present moments throughout the whole of time*. Through this consciousness of the identity of all present moments one apprehends that which is most fleeting of all, the moment, as that alone which persists. And he who, in such intuitive fashion, becomes aware that the *present*, which is in the strictest sense the sole form of reality, has its source *in us*, and thus arises from within and not from without, cannot doubt the indestructibility of his own being. He will understand, rather, that although when he dies the objective world, with the medium through which it presents itself, the intellect, will be lost to him, his existence will not be affected by it; for there has been as much reality within him as without.

Whoever does not acknowledge all this will be obliged to assert the opposite and say: 'Time is something completely objective and real which exists quite independently of me. I was only thrown into it by chance, have taken possession of a little of it and thereby attained to an ephemeral reality, as thousands of others who are now nothing have done before me, and I too shall very soon be nothing. Time, on the other hand, is what is real: it will then go on without me.' I think the fundamental perversity, indeed absurdity, of this view has only to be clearly stated to become obvious.

All this means, to be sure, that life can be regarded as a dream and death as the awakening from it: but it must be remembered that the personality, the individual, belongs to the dreaming and not to the awakened consciousness, which is why death appears to the individual as annihilation. In any event, death is not, from this point of view, to be considered a transition to a state completely new and foreign to us, but rather a return to one originally our own from which life has been only a brief absence.

Consciousness is destroyed in death, to be sure; but that which has been producing it is by no means destroyed. For consciousness depends first of all on the intellect, but the intellect depends on a physiological process: it is obviously the function of the brain and is thus conditioned by the collaboration of the nervous and vascular systems; more precisely, by the brain nourished, animated and constantly stimulated by the heart; the

brain through whose ingenious and mysterious structure, which anatomy can describe but physiology cannot
understand, there come about the phenomena of the
objective world and the workings of our thoughts. An
individual consciousness, that is to say a consciousness
of any kind, cannot be thought of apart from a *corporeal
being*, because cognition, which is the precondition of all
consciousness, is necessarily a function of the brain –
properly speaking because brain is the objective form of
intellect. Now since intellect appears physiologically, and
consequently in empirical reality, i.e. in the realm of
phenomenon, as something secondary, as a result of
the life-process, it is also secondary psychologically, in
antithesis to will, which alone is primary and everywhere
the original element. And since, therefore, consciousness
does not adhere directly to will but is conditioned by
intellect, and this last is conditioned by the organism,
there can be no doubt that consciousness is extinguished
by death – as it is by sleep or by any form of fainting or
swoon. But cheer up! – for what kind of a consciousness
is it? A cerebral, an animal, a somewhat more highly
charged bestial consciousness, in as far as we have it in
all essentials in common with the whole animal world,
even if it does reach its peak in us. This consciousness is,
in its origin and aim, merely an expedient for helping
the animal to get what it needs. The state to which death
restores us, on the other hand, is our original state, i.e.
is the being's intrinsic state, the moving principle of
which appears in the production and maintenance of the
life which is now coming to an end: it is the state of the
thing in itself, in antithesis to the world of appearance.

And in this primal state such a makeshift as cerebral, highly mediate cognition, which precisely because it is so is cognition only of phenomena, is altogether superfluous; which is precisely why we lose it. For us its abolition is one with the cessation of the world of phenomena whose mere medium it was and in which capacity alone it is of any use. Even if in this primal state we were offered the retention of this animal consciousness we should reject it, as the cured cripple rejects his crutch. Whoever therefore regrets the impending loss of this cerebral consciousness, which is adapted to and capable of producing only phenomena, is to be compared with the converts from Greenland who refused to go to Heaven when they learned there would be no seals there.

Everything said here rests, further, on the presupposition that *we* can imagine a state which is *not unconscious* only as one which is *cognisant* and moreover bears the stamp of the basic form of all cognition, the division into subject and object, into that which knows and that which is known: but we have to consider that this whole form of knowing and being known is conditioned merely by our animal nature, which is moreover very secondary and derivative, and is thus by no means the primal state of all essential being and existence, which may therefore be quite differently constituted and yet *not unconscious*. Our intrinsic actual being is, so far as we are able to penetrate it, nothing but *will*, and this is in itself without cognition. If, then, death deprives us of intellect we are thereby only transported to our *cognitionless* primal state, which is not however simply an *unconscious* state but rather one elevated above that form, a state in which the antithesis of subject and object falls away, because that which is to be known would here be actually and undividedly one with that which knows and the basic condition of all cognition (which is precisely this antithesis) would be lacking.

7

If now, instead of looking *inwards*, we again look *outwards* and take an objective view of the world which presents itself to us, then death will certainly appear to us as a transition into nothingness; on the other hand, however, birth will appear as a coming forth out of nothingness. But neither the one nor the other can be unconditionally true, for they possess the reality only of the phenomenal world. And that we should in some sense or other survive death is no greater miracle than that of procreation, which we have before our eyes every day. What dies goes to where all life originates, its own included. From this point of view our life is to be regarded as a loan received from death, with sleep as the daily interest on this loan. Death announces itself frankly as the end of the individual, but in this individual there lies the germ of a new being. Thus nothing that dies dies for ever; but nothing that is born receives a fundamentally new existence. That which dies is destroyed; but a germ remains over out of which there proceeds a new being, which then enters into existence without knowing whence it has come nor why it is as it is. This is the mystery of *palingenesis*; it reveals to us that all those beings living at the present moment contain within them

45

the actual germ of all which will live in the future, and that these therefore in a certain sense exist already. So that every animal in the full prime of life seems to call to us: 'Why do you lament the transitoriness of living things? How could I exist if all those of my species which came before me had not died?' However much the plays and the masks on the world's stage may change it is always the same actors who appear. We sit together and talk and grow excited, and our eyes glitter and our voices grow shriller: just so did *others* sit and talk a thousand years ago: it was the same thing, and it was the *same people*: and it will be just so a thousand years hence. The contrivance which prevents us from perceiving this is *time*.

One would do well to make a clear distinction between *metempsychosis*, which is the transference of the entire so-called soul into another body, and *palingenesis*, which is the *decomposition* and reconstruction of the individual in which *will* alone persists and, assuming the shape of a new being, receives a new intellect.

Throughout all time it is the male sex which stores up the will of the human species and the female which stores up the intellect. Thus each of us has a paternal and a maternal constituent; and as these are united through procreation, so they are sundered again through death, which is thus the end of the individual. It is this individual whose death we grieve so much for, in the feeling that it is really lost to us, that it was no more than a compound which has now been irretrievably broken up. Yet in all this we must not forget that the hereditariness of intellect from the mother is not so firm and unconditional as that of will from the father, the reason being the secondary and merely physical nature of intellect and its total dependence on the organism.

One can thus regard every human being from two opposed viewpoints. From the one he is the fleeting individual, burdened with error and sorrow and with a beginning and an end in time; from the other he is the indestructible primal being which is objectified in everything that exists.

8

THRASYMACHUS*: To sum up, what shall I be after my death? Be clear and precise!

PHILALETHES†: Everything and nothing.

THRASYMACHUS: As I expected! For the solution to a problem – a contradiction. That trick is very worn-out.

PHILALETHES: To answer transcendent questions in language made for immanent knowledge is bound to lead to contradictions.

THRASYMACHUS: What do you call transcendent and what immanent knowledge? – I too am familiar with these expressions; I learned them from my professor, but only as predicates of the good Lord God, with whom his philosophy was exclusively preoccupied, as was quite right and proper. If God is somewhere in the world he is immanent; but if he sits somewhere outside it, he is transcendent. – Well, that is clear, that's something you can get hold of! You

---

* Appeared in Plato's *Republic* trying to argue that 'might is right'. One of the first cultivators of rhetoric, characterized as being more concerned with winning arguments than with truth.

† Literally, 'A lover of truth'. Generic title for a philosopher.

know where you are with that. But no one can any longer understand your old-fashioned Kantian jargon. What is it supposed to mean?

PHILALETHES: Transcendent knowledge is that which, passing beyond all possible experience, strives to determine the nature of things as they are in themselves; immanent knowledge, on the other hand, is that which confines itself within the bounds of possible experience and can therefore speak only of phenomena. – You, as an individual, will come to an end with your death. But your individuality is not your essential and ultimate being, only a manifestation of it: your individuality is not the thing in itself but only the phenomenal form of it which appears under the aspect of time and consequently has a beginning and an end. Your being in itself, on the other hand, knows neither time nor beginning nor end, nor the bounds of a given individuality; thus no individuality can exclude it – it exists in everyone everywhere. In the former sense, therefore, you will when you die become nothing, in the latter everything. That is why I said that after your death you will be everything and nothing. Your question hardly permits of a better short answer than this, even though it does contain a contradiction; and it does so precisely because your life is in time but your immortality is in eternity. – Thus your immortality can also be termed an indestructibility without continued existence – which again amounts to a contradiction.

THRASYMACHUS: Well, I wouldn't give twopence for your immortality if it doesn't include the continued existence of my individuality.

PHILALETHES: But perhaps you would be willing to bargain a little. Suppose I guarantee you the continued existence of your individuality, but on condition it is preceded by a completely unconscious death-sleep of three months.

THRASYMACHUS: I would agree to that.

PHILALETHES: But since when we are completely unconscious we have no notion of the passage of time, it is all one to us whether, while we are lying in that death-sleep, three months or ten thousand years pass in the conscious world. For in either case, when we awake we have to take on trust how long we have been sleeping. So that it will be all the same to you whether your individuality is restored to you after three months or ten thousand years.

THRASYMACHUS: That cannot very well be denied.

PHILALETHES: But now, if after these ten thousand years have passed it was forgotten to wake you up, this would not, I think, be a very great misfortune, since your period of non-being would have been so long compared with your brief period of being you would have got quite used to it. What is certain, however, is that you would not have the least idea you had failed to be woken up. And you would be completely content with the whole thing if you knew that the mysterious mechanism which moves your present phenomenal form had not ceased for one moment through-out those ten thousand years to produce and move other phenomena of the same sort.

THRASYMACHUS: No, you can't cheat me out of my individuality in that way. I have stipulated that my individuality should continue to exist, and I cannot be reconciled to its loss by mechanisms and phenomena. I, I, I want to exist! *that* is what I want, and not an existence I first have to be argued into believing I possess.

PHILALETHES: But just look around you! That which cries 'I,

I, I want to exist' is not you alone; it is everything, absolutely everything that has the slightest trace of consciousness. So that this desire in you is precisely that which is *not* individual but common to everything without exception: it arises not from the individuality but from *existence* as such, is intrinsic to everything that *exists* and indeed the reason *why* it exists, and it is consequently satisfied by existence *as such*: it is this alone to which this desire applies, and not exclusively to some particular individual existence. That which desires existence so impetuously is only *indirectly* the individual! directly and intrinsically it is will to live as such, which is one and the same in all things. Since, then, existence itself is the free work, indeed the mere reflection of the will, the will cannot be deprived of it: the will is, however, temporarily satisfied by it, in so far, that is, as what is eternally unsatisfied can be satisfied at all. Individualities are a matter of indifference to the will; it is not concerned with them, although it seems to be so, because the individual has no direct knowledge of it except in himself. The effect of this is to make the individual expend more care on preserving his existence than he otherwise would, and thereby ensure the preservation of his species. From this it follows that individuality is not a form of perfection but a limitation: thus to be free of it is not a loss but rather a gain. So cease worrying about it: truly, if you knew your own being to its very depths as the universal will to live which you are – such worries would then seem to you childish and altogether ludicrous.

THRASYMACHUS: Childish and altogether ludicrous is what you yourself are, and all philosophers; and if a grown-up man like me spends fifteen minutes with fools of this kind it is merely a way of passing the time. I've now got more important things to do. Good-bye!

On Suicide

As far as I can see, it is only the monotheistic, that is to say Jewish, religions whose members regard self-destruction as a crime. This is all the more striking in that neither in the Old nor in the New Testament is there to be found any prohibition or even definite disapproval of it; so that religious teachers have to base their proscription of suicide on philosophical grounds of their own invention, which are however so poor that what their arguments lack in strength they have to try to make up for by the strength of the terms in which they express their abhorrence; that is to say, they resort to abuse. Thus we hear that suicide is the most cowardly of acts, that only a madman would commit it, and similar insipidities; or the senseless assertion that suicide is 'wrong', though it is obvious there is nothing in the world a man has a more incontestable *right* to than his own life and person. Let us for once allow moral feelings to decide this question, and compare the impression made on us by the news that an acquaintance of ours has committed a crime, for instance a murder, an act of cruelty, a betrayal, a theft, with that produced by the news that he has voluntarily ended his life. While the former will evoke a lively indignation, anger, the demand for punishment or revenge, the latter will excite pity and sorrow, which are more likely to be accompanied by admiration for his courage than by moral disapproval. Who has not had acquaintances, friends, relatives who have departed this world voluntarily? – and is one supposed to think of them with repugnance, as if they were criminals? In my opinion it ought rather to be demanded of the clergy that they tell us by what authority they go to their pulpits or their desks and brand as a *crime* an action which many people we honour and love have performed and deny an honourable burial to those who have departed this world voluntarily – since they cannot point to a single biblical authority, nor produce a single sound philosophical argument; it being made clear that what one wants are *reasons* and not empty phrases or abuse. If the criminal law proscribes suicide this is no valid reason for the Church to do so, and is moreover a decidedly ludicrous proceeding, for what punishment can deter him who is looking for death? If one punishes attempted suicide, it is the ineptitude of the attempt one punishes.

The only cogent moral argument against suicide is that it is opposed to the achievement of the highest moral goal, inasmuch as it substitutes for a true redemption from this world of misery a merely apparent one. But it is a very long way from a mistake of this kind to a crime, which is what the Christian clergy want to call it.

Christianity carries in its innermost heart the truth that suffering (the Cross) is the true aim of life: that is why it repudiates suicide, which is opposed to this aim, while antiquity from a lower viewpoint approved of and indeed honoured it. This argument against suicide is however an ascetic one, and is therefore valid only from a far higher ethical standpoint than any which European moral philosophers have ever assumed. If we descend from this very high standpoint there no longer remains any tenable moral reason for damning suicide. It therefore seems that the extraordinary zeal in opposing it displayed by the clergy of monotheistic religions – a zeal which is not supported by the Bible or by any cogent reasons – must have some hidden reason behind it: may this not be that the voluntary surrender of life is an ill compliment to him who said that all things were very good? If so, it is another instance of the obligatory optimism of these religions, which denounces self-destruction so as not to be denounced by it.

2

It will generally be found that where the terrors of life come to outweigh the terrors of death a man will put an end to his life. But the terrors of death offer considerable resistance: they stand like a sentinel at the exit gate. Perhaps there is no one alive who would not already have put an end to his life if this end were something purely negative, a sudden cessation of existence. But there is something positive in it as well: the destruction of the body. This is a deterrent, because the body is the phenomenal form of the will to live.

The struggle with that sentinel is as a rule, however, not as hard as it may seem to us from a distance: the reason is the antagonism between spiritual and physical suffering. For when we are in great or chronic physical pain we are indifferent to all other troubles: all we are concerned about is recovering. In the same way, great spiritual suffering makes us insensible to physical pain: we despise it: indeed, if it should come to outweigh the other it becomes a beneficial distraction, an interval in spiritual suffering. It is this which makes suicide easier: for the physical pain associated with it loses all significance in the eyes of one afflicted by excessive spiritual suffering.

On Women

I

Schiller's whole comprehensive poem *Würde der Frauen*, with its effects of antithesis and contrast, fails, in my opinion, to express what is truly to be praised in women as well as do these few words of Jouy:* *Sans les femmes, le commencement de notre vie serait privé de secours, le milieu de plaisirs, et la fin de consolation.†* Byron says the same thing with more pathos in *Sardanapolis.‡*

> The very first
> Of human life must spring from woman's breast,
> Your first small words are taught you from her lips,
> Your first tears quench'd by her, and your last sighs
> Too often breathed out in a woman's hearing,
> When men have shrunk from the ignoble care
> Of watching the last hour of him who led them.

---

*Johann Christoph Friedrich von Schiller (1759–1805) is traditionally Germany's second greatest poet, but much of his verse, of which *The Dignity* (or Merit or Worth) *of Women* is a once-famous example, is of the 'good bad' variety, like Walter Scott's. His true genius lay in the field of popular drama, and his best plays are still much performed. Victor Jouy (1764–1846), dramatist.

†Without women, the beginning of our lives would be deprived of security, the middle of pleasure, and the end of consolation.

‡Act I, scene 2.

Both indicate the correct viewpoint for estimating the value of women.

2

One needs only to see the way she is built to realize that woman is not intended for great mental or for great physical labour. She expiates the guilt of life not through activity but through suffering, through the pains of child-birth, caring for the child and subjection to the man, to whom she should be a patient and cheering companion. Great suffering, joy, exertion, is not for her: her life should flow by more quietly, trivially, gently than the man's without being essentially happier or unhappier.

3

Women are suited to being the nurses and teachers of our earliest childhood precisely because they themselves are childish, silly and short-sighted, in a word big children, their whole lives long: a kind of intermediate stage between the child and the man, who is the actual human being, 'man'. One has only to watch a girl playing with a child, dancing and singing with it the whole day, and then ask oneself what, with the best will in the world, a man could do in her place.

4

In the girl nature has had in view what could in theatrical terms be called a stage-effect: it has provided her with superabundant beauty and charm for a few years at the expense of the whole remainder of her life, so that during these years she may so capture the imagination of a man that he is carried away into undertaking to support her honourably in some form or another for the rest of her life, a step he would seem hardly likely to take for purely rational considerations. Thus nature has equipped women, as it has all its creatures, with the tools and weapons she needs for securing her existence, and at just the time she needs them; in doing which nature has acted with its usual economy. For just as the female ant loses its wings after mating, since they are then superfluous, indeed harmful to the business of raising the family, so the woman usually loses her beauty after one or two childbeds, and probably for the same reason.

5

The nobler and more perfect a thing is, the later and more slowly does it mature. The man attains the maturity of his reasoning powers and spiritual faculties hardly before his twenty-eighth year; the woman with her eighteenth. And even then it is only reasoning power of a sort: a very limited sort. Thus women remain children all their lives, never see anything but what is closest to them, cleave to the present moment, take appearance for reality and prefer trifles to the most important affairs. For reason is the faculty by virtue of which man lives not merely in the present, as the animal does, but surveys and ponders past and future, from which arises his capacity for foresight, his care and trouble, and the anxiety he so frequently feels. As a consequence of her weaker reasoning powers, woman has a smaller share of the advantages and disadvantages these bring with them: she is, rather, a mental myopic, in that her intuitive understanding sees very clearly what is close to her but has a very narrow field of vision from which what is distant is excluded; so that what is absent, past or to come makes a very much weaker impression on women than it does on us, which is the origin of their much greater tendency to squandering, a tendency which sometimes verges on madness. Women think in their hearts that the man's business is to make money and theirs is to spend it: where possible during the man's lifetime, but in any case after his death. That the man hands over to them for housekeeping the money he has earned strengthens them in this belief. – Whatever disadvantages all this may bring with it, it has this good effect, that woman is more absorbed in the present than we are, so that, if the present is endurable at all, she enjoys it more, and this produces that cheerfulness characteristic of her through which she is so suited to entertain and, if need be, console the care-laden man.

To consult women when you are in difficulties, as the ancient Teutons did, is by no means a bad idea: for their way of looking at things is quite different from ours, especially in their propensity for keeping in view the shortest road to a desired goal and in general what lies closest to hand, which we usually overlook precisely because it is right in front of our noses. In addition, women are decidedly more prosaic than we are and see no more in things than is really there, while we, if our passions are aroused, will easily exaggerate and indulge in imaginings.

It is for this reason too that women display more pity, and consequently more philanthropy and sympathy with the unfortunate, than men do; on the other hand, they are inferior to men in respect of justice, honesty and conscientiousness: for as a result of their weaker reasoning power women are as a rule far more affected by what is present, visible and immediately real than they are by abstract ideas, standing maxims, previous decisions or in general by regard for what is far off, in the past or still to come. Thus, while they possess the first and chief virtue, they are deficient in the secondary one which is often necessary for achieving the first. – One must accordingly say that the fundamental defect of the female character is *a lack of a sense of justice*. This originates first and foremost in their want of rationality and capacity for reflexion but it is strengthened by the fact that, as the weaker sex, they are driven to rely not on force but on cunning: hence their instinctive subtlety and their ineradicable tendency to tell lies: for, as nature has equipped the lion with claws and teeth, the elephant with tusks, the wild boar with fangs, the bull with horns and the cuttlefish with ink, so it has equipped woman with the power of dissimulation as her means of attack and defence, and has transformed into this gift all the strength it has bestowed on man in the form of physical strength and the power of reasoning. Dissimulation is thus inborn in her and consequently to be found in the stupid woman almost as often as in the clever one. To make use of it at every opportunity is as natural to her as it is for an animal to employ its means of defence whenever it is attacked, and when she does so she feels that to some extent she is only exercising her rights. A completely truthful woman who does not practise dissimulation is perhaps an impossibility, which is why women see through the dissimulation of others so easily it is inadvisable to attempt it with them. – But this fundamental defect which I have said they possess, together with all that is associated with it, gives rise to falsity, unfaithfulness, treachery, ingratitude, etc. Women are guilty of perjury far more often than men. It is questionable whether they ought to be allowed to take an oath at all.

6

To take care of the propagation of the human race nature has chosen the young, strong and handsome men, so that the race shall not degenerate. This is the firm will of nature in this matter, and its expression is the passion of women. In antiquity and force this law precedes every other: so woe to him who sets his rights and interests in the path of this law: whatever he says or does they will, at the first serious encounter, be mercilessly crushed. For the secret, unspoken, indeed unconscious, but nonetheless inborn morality of women is: 'We are justified in deceiving those who, because they provide a meagre support for us, the individual, think they have acquired a right over the species. The character and consequently the well-being of the species has, through the next generation proceeding from us, been placed in our hands and entrusted to our care: let us discharge that trust conscientiously.' Women are, however, by no means conscious of this supreme law *in abstracto*,* only *in*

* In abstract, by means of concepts.

concreto;* and they have no way of giving expression to it apart from their mode of action if the occasion presents itself; and then they are usually less troubled by their conscience than we suppose, because they are aware in the darkest recesses of their heart that in violating their duty to the individual they are all the better fulfilling their duty to the species, whose rights are incomparably greater.

Because fundamentally women exist solely for the propagation of the race and find in this their entire vocation, they are altogether more involved with the species than with individuals, and in their hearts take the affairs of the species more seriously than they do those of the individual. This gives their entire nature and all their activities a certain levity and in general a direction fundamentally different from those of the man: which is why dissension between married couples is so frequent and indeed almost the normal case.

7

Men are by nature merely indifferent to one another; but women are by nature enemies. The reason is no doubt that that *odium figulinum*† which with men does not go beyond the bounds of the particular guild, with women embraces the whole sex, because they are all engaged in the same trade. Even when they simply pass in the street they look at one another like Guelphs and Ghibellines; and when two women meet for the first

* By individual intuition.
† Mutual dislike of those in the same trade.

time there is clearly more constraint and pretence involved than in the case of two men: so that when two women exchange compliments it sounds much more ludicrous than when two men do so. Further, while a man will as a rule still preserve some degree of consideration and humanity even when addressing men very much his inferior, it is intolerable to see with what haughty disdain an aristocratic woman usually speaks to women who are beneath her (I am not referring to servants). The reason for this may be that with women all differences in rank are far more precarious than they are with us, and can be altered or abolished much more quickly, because in our case a hundred different considerations are involved, while in theirs only one is decisive, namely which man they have succeeded in attracting. Another reason may be that, because they are all in the same profession, they all stand much closer to one another than men do, and consequently strive to emphasize differences in rank.

8

Only a male intellect clouded by the sexual drive could call the stunted, narrow-shouldered, broad-hipped and short-legged sex the fair sex: for it is with this drive that all its beauty is bound up. More fittingly than the fair sex, women could be called the *unaesthetic* sex. Neither for music, nor poetry, nor the plastic arts do they possess any real feeling or receptivity: if they affect to do so, it is merely mimicry in service of their effort to please. This comes from the fact that they are incapable of taking a *purely objective interest* in anything whatever, and the reason for this is, I think, as follows. Man strives in everything for a *direct* domination over things, either by comprehending or by subduing them. But woman is everywhere and always relegated to a merely *indirect* domination, which is achieved by means of man, who is consequently the only thing she has to dominate directly. Thus it lies in the nature of women to regard everything simply as a means of capturing a man, and their interest in anything else is only simulated, is no more than a detour, i.e. amounts to coquetry and mimicry. One has only to observe how they behave in the theatre or at operas and concerts, e.g. the childish unconcern with which they go on chattering away during the most beautiful parts of the greatest masterpieces. If it is true the Greeks refused to allow women into the theatre, they did the right thing: at least one would have been able to hear what was going on. – Nor can one expect anything else from women if one considers that the most eminent heads of the entire sex have proved incapable of a single truly great, genuine and original achievement in art, or indeed of creating anything at all of lasting value: this strikes one most forcibly in regard to painting, since they are just as capable of mastering its technique as we are, and indeed paint very busily, yet cannot point to a single great painting; the reason being precisely that they lack all objectivity of mind, which is what painting demands above all else. Isolated and partial exceptions do not alter the case: women, taken as a whole, are and remain thorough and incurable philistines: so that, with the extremely absurd arrangement by which they share the rank and title of their husband, they are a continual

spur to his *ignoble* ambitions. They are *sexus sequior*,*
the inferior second sex in *every* respect: one should be
indulgent towards their weaknesses, but to pay them
honour is ridiculous beyond measure and demeans us
even in their eyes. – This is how the peoples of antiquity
and of the Orient have regarded women; they have
recognized what is the proper position for women far
better than we have, we with our Old French gallantry
and insipid women-veneration, that highest flower of
Christian-Germanic stupidity which has served only to
make women so rude and arrogant that one is sometimes
reminded of the sacred apes of Benares which, conscious
of their own sanctity and inviolability, thought themselves at liberty to do whatever they pleased.

Woman in the Occident, that is to say the 'lady', finds
herself in a false position: for woman is by no means
fitted to be the object of our veneration, to hold her
head higher than the man or to enjoy equal rights with
him. The consequences of this false position are
sufficiently obvious. It would thus be a very desirable
thing if this number two of the human race were again
put in her natural place in Europe too, and a limit set to
the unnaturalness called a lady at which all Asia laughs
and which Greece and Rome would laugh at too if they
could see it: the consequences for the social, civil and
political life of Europe would be incalculably beneficial.
The European lady is a creature which ought not to exist
at all: what there ought to be is housewives and girls
who hope to become housewives and who are therefore

* The second sex, the inferior sex.

educated, not in arrogant haughtiness, but in domesticity and submissiveness. It is precisely because there are *ladies* that European women of a lower status, which is to say the great majority of the sex, are much more unhappy than they are in the Orient.

9

In our monogamous part of the world, to marry means to have one's rights and double one's duties. But when the law conceded women equal rights with men it should at the same time have endowed them with masculine reasoning powers. What is actually the case is that the more those rights and privileges the law accords to women exceed those which are natural to them, the more it reduces the number of women who actually participate in these benefits; and then the remainder are deprived of their natural rights by just the amount these few receive in excess of theirs: for, because of the unnaturally privileged position enjoyed by women as a consequence of monogamy and the marriage laws accompanying it, which regard women as entirely equal to men (which they are in no respect), prudent and cautious men very often hesitate before making so great a sacrifice as is involved in entering into so inequitable a contract; so that while among polygamous peoples every woman gets taken care of, among the monogamous the number of married women is limited and there remains over a quantity of unsupported women who, in the upper classes, vegetate on as useless old maids, and in the lower are obliged to undertake laborious work they are constitutionally unfitted for or become *filles de joie*,* whose lives are as devoid of *joie*† as they are of honour but who, given the prevailing circumstances, are necessary for the gratification of the male sex and therefore come to constitute a recognized class, with the specific task of preserving the virtue of those women more favoured by fate who have found a man to support them or may reasonably hope to find one. There are 80,000 prostitutes in London alone: and what are they if not sacrifices on the altar of monogamy? These poor women are the inevitable counterpart and natural complement to the European lady, with all her arrogance and pretension. For the female sex viewed *as a whole* polygamy is therefore a real benefit; on the other hand there appears no rational ground why a man whose wife suffers from a chronic illness, or has remained unfruitful, or has gradually grown too old for him, should not take a second.

There can be no argument about polygamy: it is a fact to be met with everywhere, and the only question is how to *regulate* it. For who is really a monogamist? We all live in polygamy, *at least* for a time and usually for good. Since every man needs many women, there could be nothing more just than that he should be free, indeed obliged, to support many women. This would also mean the restoration of woman to her rightful and natural position, the subordinate one, and the abolition from the world of the *lady*, with her ridiculous claims to respect and veneration; there would then be only *women*, and no longer *unhappy women*, of which Europe is at present full.

---

* Prostitutes.   † Joy, or happiness.

On Thinking for Yourself

As the biggest library if it is in disorder is not as useful as a small but well-arranged one, so you may accumulate a vast amount of knowledge but it will be of far less value to you than a much smaller amount if you have not thought it over for yourself; because only through ordering what you know by comparing every truth with every other truth can you take complete possession of your knowledge and get it into your power. You can think about only what you know, so you ought to learn something; on the other hand, you can know only what you have thought about.

Now you can apply yourself voluntarily to reading and learning, but you cannot really apply yourself to thinking: thinking has to be kindled, as a fire is by a draught, and kept going by some kind of interest in its object, which may be an objective interest or merely a subjective one. The latter is possible only with things that affect us personally, the former only to those heads who think by nature, to whom thinking is as natural as breathing, and these are very rare. That is why most scholars do so little of it.

2

The difference between the effect produced on the mind by thinking for yourself and that produced by reading is incredibly great, so that the original difference which made one head decide for thinking and another for reading is continually increased. For reading forcibly imposes on the mind thoughts that are as foreign to its mood and direction at the moment of reading as the signet is to the wax upon which it impresses its seal. The mind is totally subjected to an external compulsion to think this or that for which it has no inclination and is not in the mood. On the other hand, when it is thinking for itself it is following its own inclination, as this has been more closely determined either by its immediate surroundings or by some recollection or other: for its visible surroundings do not impose some *single* thought on the mind, as reading does; they merely provide it with occasion and matter for thinking the thoughts appropriate to its nature and present mood. The result is that *much* reading robs the mind of all elasticity, as the continual pressure of a weight does a spring, and that the surest way of never having any thoughts of your own is to pick up a book every time you have a free moment. The practice of doing this is the reason erudition makes most men duller and sillier than they are by nature and robs their writings of all effectiveness: they are in Pope's words:

For ever reading, never to be read.

3

Fundamentally it is only our own basic thoughts that possess truth and life, for only these do we really understand through and through. The thoughts of another that we have read are crumbs from another's table, the cast-off clothes of an unfamiliar guest.

4

Reading is merely a surrogate for thinking for yourself; it means letting someone else direct your thoughts. Many books, moreover, serve merely to show how many ways there are of being wrong, and how far astray you yourself would go if you followed their guidance. – You should read only when your own thoughts dry up, which will of course happen frequently enough even to the best heads; but to banish your own thoughts so as to take up a book is a sin against the Holy Ghost; it is like deserting untrammelled nature to look at a herbarium or engravings of landscapes.

It may sometimes happen that a truth, an insight, which you have slowly and laboriously puzzled out by thinking for yourself could easily have been found already written in a book; but it is a hundred times more valuable if you have arrived at it by thinking for yourself. For only then will it enter your thought-system as an integral part and living member, be perfectly and firmly consistent with it and in accord with all its other consequences and conclusions, bear the hue, colour and stamp of your whole manner of thinking, and have arrived at just the moment it was needed; thus it will stay firmly and for ever lodged in your mind. This is a perfect application, indeed explanation, of Goethe's lines:

> Was du ererbt von deinen Vätern hast,
> Erwirb es, um es zu besitzen.*

For the man who thinks for himself becomes acquainted with the authorities for his opinions only after he has acquired them and merely as a confirmation of them, while the book-philosopher starts with his authorities, in that he constructs his opinions by collecting together the opinions of others: his mind then compares with that of the former as an automaton compares with a living man.

A truth that has merely been learnt adheres to us only as an artificial limb, a false tooth, a wax nose does, or at most like transplanted skin; but a truth won by thinking for ourself is like a natural limb: it alone really belongs to us. This is what determines the difference between a thinker and a mere scholar.

5

People who pass their lives in reading and acquire their wisdom from books are like those who learn about a country from travel descriptions: they can impart information about a great number of things, but at bottom they possess no connected, clear, thorough knowledge of what the country is like. On the other hand, people

---

* What you have inherited from your forefathers you must first win for yourself if you are to possess it.

who pass their lives in thinking are like those who have visited the country themselves: they alone are really familiar with it, possess connected knowledge of it and are truly at home in it.

6

A man who thinks for himself is related to the ordinary book-philosopher as an eyewitness is to an historian: the former speaks from his own immediate experience. That is why all men who think for themselves are in fundamental agreement: their differences spring only from their differing standpoints; for they merely express what they have objectively apprehended. The book-philosopher, on the contrary, reports what this man has said and that has thought and the other has objected, etc. Then he compares, weighs, criticizes these statements, and thus tries to get to the truth of the matter, in which respect he exactly resembles the critical historian.

7

Mere experience is no more a substitute for thinking than reading is. Pure empiricism is related to thinking as eating is to digestion and assimilation. When empiricism boasts that it alone has, through its discoveries, advanced human knowledge, it is as if the mouth should boast that it alone keeps the body alive.

8

The characteristic mark of minds of the first rank is the immediacy of all their judgements. Everything they produce is the result of thinking for themselves and already in the way it is spoken everywhere announces itself as such. He who truly thinks for himself is like a monarch, in that he recognizes no one over him. His judgements, like the decisions of a monarch, arise directly from his own absolute power. He no more accepts authorities than a monarch does orders, and he acknowledges the validity of nothing he has not himself confirmed.

9

In the realm of actuality, however fair, happy and pleasant we may find it, we are nonetheless always under the influence of gravity, which we have continually to overcome: in the realm of thought, on the contrary, we are disembodied minds, weightless and without needs or cares. That is why there is no happiness on earth to compare with that which a beautiful and fruitful mind finds in a propitious hour in itself.

10

There are very many thoughts which have value for him who thinks them, but only a few of them possess the power of engaging the interest of a reader after they have been written down.

11

Yet, all the same, only that possesses true value which you have thought in the first instance *for your own instruction*. Thinkers can be divided into those who think in the first instance for their own instruction and those who do so for the instruction of others. The former are genuine *thinkers for themselves* in both senses of the words: they are the true *philosophers*. They alone are in earnest. The pleasure and happiness of their existence consists in thinking. The latter are *sophists*: they want to *appear* as thinkers and seek their happiness in what they hope thereby to get from others. This is what they are in earnest about. To which of these two classes a man belongs may quickly be seen by his whole style and manner. Lichtenberg is an example of the former class, Herder certainly belongs to the latter.*

12

When you consider how great and how immediate is the *problem of existence*, this ambiguous, tormented, fleeting, dream-like existence – so great and so immediate that as soon as you are aware of it it overshadows and obscures all other problems and aims; and when you then see how men, with a few rare exceptions, have no clear awareness of this problem, indeed seem not to be conscious of it at all, but concern themselves with anything rather than with this problem and live on taking thought only for the day and for the hardly longer span of their own individual future, either expressly refusing to consider this problem or contenting themselves with some system of popular metaphysics; when, I say, you consider this, you may come to the opinion that man can be called a *thinking being* only in a very broad sense of that term and no longer feel very much surprise at any

* Georg Christoph Lichtenberg (1742–99), aphorist and satirist. Johann Gottfried von Herder (1744–1803), theologian, philosopher and man of letters.

thoughtlessness or silliness whatever, but will realize, rather, that while the intellectual horizon of the normal man is wider than that of the animal – whose whole existence is, as it were, one continual present, with no consciousness of past or future – it is not so immeasurably wider as is generally supposed.

APHORISMS

On Philosophy and the Intellect

The fundament upon which all our knowledge and learning rests is the inexplicable. It is to this that every explanation, through few or many intermediate stages, leads; as the plummet touches the bottom of the sea now at a greater depth, now at a less, but is bound to reach it somewhere sooner or later. The study of this inexplicable devolves upon metaphysics.

2

For *intellect in the service of will*, that is to say in practical use, there exist only *individual things*; for intellect engaged in art and science, that is to say active for its own sake, there exist only *universals*, entire kinds, species, classes, *ideas* of things. Even the sculptor, in depicting the individual, seeks to depict the idea, the species. The reason for this is that *will* aims directly only at individual things, which are its true objective, for only they possess empirical reality. Concepts, classes, kinds, on the other hand, can become its objective only very indirectly. That is why the ordinary man has no sense for general truths, and why the genius, on the contrary, overlooks and neglects what is individual: to the genius the enforced occupation with the individual as such which constitutes the stuff of practical life is a burdensome drudgery.

3

The two main requirements for philosophizing are: firstly, to have the courage not to keep any question back; and secondly, to attain a clear consciousness of anything that *goes without saying* so as to comprehend it as a problem. Finally, the mind must, if it is really to philosophize, also be truly disengaged: it must prosecute no particular goal or aim, and thus be free from the enticement of will, but devote itself undividedly to the instruction which the perceptible world and its own consciousness imparts to it.

4

The *poet* presents the imagination with images from life and human characters and situations, sets them all in motion and leaves it to the beholder to let these images take his thoughts as far as his mental powers will permit. That is why he is able to engage men of the most differing capabilities, indeed fools and sages together. The *philosopher*, on the other hand, presents not life itself but the finished thoughts which he has abstracted from it and then demands that the reader should think precisely as, and precisely as far as, he himself thinks. That is why his public is so small. The poet can thus be compared with one who presents flowers, the philosopher with one who presents their essence.

5

An odd and unworthy definition of philosophy, which however even Kant gives, is that it is a science *composed* *only of concepts*. For the entire property of a concept consists of nothing more than what has been begged and borrowed from perceptual knowledge, which is the true and inexhaustible source of all insight. So that a true philosophy cannot be spun out of mere abstract concepts, but has to be founded on observation and experience, inner and outer. Nor will anything worthwhile be achieved in philosophy by synthesizing experiments with concepts such as have been performed so often in the past but especially by the sophists of our own day – I mean by Fichte and Schelling and even more offensively by Hegel, and in the field of ethics by Schleiermacher.* Philosophy, just as much as art and poetry, must have its source in perceptual comprehension of the world: nor, however much the head needs to remain on top, ought it to be so cold-blooded a business that the whole man, heart and head, is not finally involved and affected through and through. Philosophy is not algebra: on the contrary, Vauvenargues† was right when he said: *Les grandes pensées viennent du cœur*.‡

* Johann Gottlieb Fichte (1762–1814), Friedrich Wilhelm Joseph von Schelling (1775–1854), Georg Wilhelm Friedrich Hegel (1770–1831): German philosophers, the most influential of their age and the subject of constant attack by Schopenhauer. Friedrich Ernst Daniel Schleiermacher (1768–1834), theologian: when Schopenhauer attacks 'Rationalism' in religion it is Schleiermacher he has in mind.
† Luc de Clapiers, Marquis de Vauvenargues (1715–47), 'moralist' in the French sense.
‡ Great thoughts spring from the heart.

6

Mere subtlety may qualify you as a sceptic but not as a philosopher. On the other hand, scepticism is in philosophy what the Opposition is in Parliament; it is just as beneficial, and indeed necessary. It rests everywhere on the fact that philosophy is not capable of producing the kind of evidence mathematics produces.

7

A *dictate of reason* is the name we give to certain propositions which we hold true without investigation and of which we think ourselves so firmly convinced we should be incapable of seriously testing them even if we wanted to, since we should then have to call them provisionally in doubt. We credit these propositions so completely because when we first began to speak and think we continually had them recited to us and they were thus implanted in us; so that the habit of thinking them is as old as the habit of thinking as such and we can no longer separate the two.

8

People never weary of reproaching metaphysics with the very small progress it has made compared with the very great progress of the physical sciences. But what other science has been hampered at all times by having an antagonist *ex officio*, a public prosecutor, a king's champion in full armour against it? Metaphysics will never put forth its full powers so long as it is expected to accommodate itself to dogma. The various religions have taken possession of the metaphysical tendency of mankind, partly by paralysing it through imprinting their dogmas upon it in the earliest years, partly by forbidding and proscribing all free and uninhibited expression of it; so that free investigation of man's most important and interesting concern, of his existence itself, has been in part indirectly hampered, in part made subjectively impossible by the paralysis referred to; and in this way his most sublime tendency has been put in chains.

9

The discovery of truth is prevented most effectively, not by the false appearance things present and which mislead into error, nor directly by weakness of the reasoning powers, but by preconceived opinion, by prejudice, which as a pseudo *a priori* stands in the path of truth and is then like a contrary wind driving a ship away from land, so that sail and rudder labour in vain.

10

Every *general* truth is related to specific truths as gold is to silver, inasmuch as it can be converted into a considerable number of specific truths which follow from it in the same way as a gold coin can be converted into small change.

11

From *one* proposition nothing more can follow than what is already contained in it, i.e. than what it itself implies when its meaning is exhausted; but from *two* propositions, if they are joined together as premises of a syllogism, more can follow than is contained in either of them taken individually – just as a body formed by chemical combination exhibits qualities possessed by none of its constituents. That logical conclusions possess value derives from this fact.

12

What light is to the outer physical world intellect is to the inner world of consciousness. For intellect is related to will, and thus also to the organism, which is nothing other than will regarded objectively, in approximately the same way as light is to a combustible body and the oxygen in combination with which it ignites. And as light is the purer the less it is involved with the smoke of the burning body, so also is intellect the purer the more completely it is separated from the will which engendered it. In a bolder metaphor one could even say: Life is known to be a process of combustion; intellect is the light produced by this process.

13

The simplest unprejudiced self-observation, combined with the facts of anatomy, leads to the conclusion that intellect, like its objectivization the brain, is, together with its dependent sense-apparatus, nothing other than a very intense receptivity to influences from without and does not constitute our original and intrinsic being; thus that intellect is not that in us which in a plant is motive power or in a stone weight and chemical forces: it is *will* alone which appears in these forms. Intellect is that in us which in a plant is merely receptivity to external

influences, to physical and chemical action and whatever
else may help or hinder it to grow and thrive; but in us
this receptivity has risen to such a pitch of intensity that
by virtue of it the entire objective world, the world as
idea, appears; and this, consequently, is how its objectivization originates. It will help to make all this more vivid
if you imagine the world without any animal life on it.
There will then be nothing on it capable of perceiving
it, and therefore it will actually have no objective existence at all. Now imagine a number of plants shooting
up out of the ground close beside one another. All kinds
of things will begin to operate on them, such as air, wind,
the pressure of one plant against another, moisture,
cold, light, warmth, electricity, etc. Now imagine the
receptivity of these plants to influences of this kind
intensified more and more: it will finally become sensation, accompanied by the capacity to refer sensation
to its cause, and at last perception: whereupon the world
will be there, appearing in space, time and causal connexion – yet it will still be merely the result of external
influences on the receptivity of the plants. This pictorial
representation brings home very well the merely
phenomenal existence of the external world and makes
it comprehensible: for no one, surely, would care to
assert that a state of affairs which consists of perceptions
originating in nothing but relations between external
influences and active receptivity represents the truly
objective, inner and original constitution of all those
natural forces assumed to be acting on the plants; that it
represents, that is to say, the world of things in themselves. This picture can thus make it comprehensible to

us why the realm of the human intellect should have such narrow boundaries, as Kant demonstrates it has in the *Critique of Pure Reason*.

14

That you should write down valuable ideas that occur to you as soon as possible goes without saying: we sometimes forget even what we have done, so how much more what we have thought. Thoughts, however, come not when *we* but when *they* want. On the other hand, it is better not to copy down what we have received finished and complete from without, what we have merely learned and what can in any case be discovered again in books: for to copy something down is to consign it to forgetfulness. You should deal sternly and despotically with your memory, so that it does not unlearn obedience; if, for example, you cannot call something to mind, a line of poetry or a word perhaps, you should not go and look it up in a book, but periodically plague your memory with it for weeks on end until your memory has done its duty. For the longer you have had to rack your brains for something the more firmly will it stay once you have got it.

15

The *quality* of our thoughts (their formal value) comes from within, their *direction*, and thus their matter, from without; so that what we are thinking at any given moment is the product of two fundamentally different factors. Consequently, the object of thought is to the mind only what the plectrum is to the lyre: which is why the same sight inspires such very different thoughts in differing heads.

16

How very paltry and limited the normal human intellect is, and how little lucidity there is in the human consciousness, may be judged from the fact that, despite the ephemeral brevity of human life, the uncertainty of our existence and the countless enigmas which press upon us from all sides, everyone does not continually and ceaselessly philosophize, but that only the rarest of exceptions do so. The rest live their lives away in this dream not very differently from the animals, from which they are in the end distinguished only by their ability to provide for a few years ahead. If they should ever feel any metaphysical need, it is taken care of from above and in advance by the various religions; and these, whatever they may be like, suffice.

17

One might almost believe that half our thinking takes place unconsciously. Usually we arrive at a conclusion without having clearly thought about the premises which lead to it. This is already evident from the fact that sometimes an occurrence whose consequences we can in no way foresee, still less clearly estimate its possible influence on our own affairs, will nonetheless exercise an unmistakable influence on our whole mood and will change it from cheerful to sad or from sad to cheerful: this can only be the result of unconscious rumination. It is even more obvious in the following: I have familiarized myself with the factual data of a theoretical or practical problem; I do not think about it again, yet often a few days later the answer to the problem will come into my mind entirely of its own accord; the operation which has produced it, however, remains as much a mystery to me as that of an adding-machine: what has occurred is, again, unconscious rumination. – One might almost venture the physiological hypothesis that conscious thinking takes place on the surface of the brain, unconscious thinking inside it.

18

Considering the monotony and consequent insipidity of life one would find it unendurably tedious after any considerable length of time, were it not for the continual advance of knowledge and insight and the acquisition of even better and clearer understanding of all things, which is partly the fruit of experience, partly the result of the changes we ourselves undergo through the different stages of life by which our point of view is to a certain extent being continually altered, whereby things reveal to us sides we did not yet know. In this way, despite the decline in our mental powers, *dies diem docet** still holds indefatigably true and gives life an ever-renewed fascination, in that what is identical continually appears as something new and different.

19

It is quite natural that we should adopt a defensive and negative attitude towards every new opinion concerning

* 'The day teaches the day' – there is something new every day.

something on which we have already an opinion of our own. For it forces its way as an enemy into the previously closed system of our own convictions, shatters the calm of mind we have attained through this system, demands renewed efforts of us and declares our former efforts to have been in vain. A truth which retrieves us from error is consequently to be compared with a physic, as much for its bitter and repellent taste as for the fact that it takes effect not at the moment it is imbibed but only some time afterwards.

Thus, if we see the individual obstinately clinging to his errors, with the mass of men it is even worse: once they have acquired an opinion, experience and instruction can labour for centuries against it and labour in vain. So that there exist certain universally popular and firmly accredited errors which countless numbers contentedly repeat every day: I have started a list of them which others might like to continue.

1. Suicide is a cowardly act.
2. He who mistrusts others is himself dishonest.
3. Worth and genius are unfeignedly modest.
4. The insane are exceedingly unhappy.
5. Philosophizing can be learned, but not philosophy. (The opposite is true.)
6. It is easier to write a good tragedy than a good comedy.
7. A little philosophy leads away from God, a lot of it leads back to him – repeated after Francis Bacon.
8. Knowledge is power. The devil it is! One man can have a great deal of knowledge without its giving him the

least power, while another possesses supreme authority but next to no knowledge.

Most of these are repeated parrot fashion without much thought being given to them and merely because when people first heard them said they found them very wise-sounding.

20

Intellect is a magnitude of intensity, not a magnitude of extension: which is why in this respect one man can confidently take on ten thousand and a thousand fools do not make one wise man.

21

What the pathetic commonplace heads with which the world is crammed really lack are two closely related faculties: that of forming judgements and that of producing ideas of their own. But these are lacking to a degree which he who is not one of them cannot easily conceive, so that he cannot easily conceive the dolefulness of their existence. It is this deficiency, however, which explains on one hand the poverty of the scribbling which in all nations passes itself off to its contemporaries as their literature, and on the other the fate that overtakes true and genuine men who appear among such people. All genuine thought and art is to a certain extent an attempt to put big heads on small people: so it is no wonder the attempt does not always come off. For a writer to afford enjoyment always demands a certain *harmony* between his way of thinking and that of the reader; and the enjoyment will be the greater the more perfect this harmony is: so that a great mind will fully and completely enjoy only another great mind. It is for this same reason that bad or mediocre writers excite disgust and revulsion in thinking heads: and even conversation with most people has the same effect – one is conscious of the inadequacy and *disharmony* every step of the way.

22

The life of the *plants* consists in simple *existence*: so that their enjoyment of life is a purely and absolutely subjective, torpid contentment. With the *animals* there enters *knowledge*: but it is still entirely restricted to what serves their own motivation, and indeed their most immediate motivation. That is why they too find complete contentment in simple existence and why it suffices to fill their entire lives; so that they can pass many hours completely inactive without feeling discontented or impatient, although they are not thinking but merely looking. Only in the very cleverest animals such as dogs and apes does the need for activity, and with that boredom, make itself felt; which is why they enjoy playing, and why they amuse themselves by gazing at passers-by; in which respect they are in a class with those human window gazers who stare at us everywhere but only when one notices they are students really arouse our indignation.

Only in man has *knowledge* – i.e. the consciousness of other things, in antithesis to mere self-consciousness – reached a high degree and, with the appearance of the reasoning faculty, risen to thought. As a consequence of this his life can, besides simple existence, be filled by *knowledge* as such, which is to a certain extent a second existence outside oneself in other beings and things. With man too, however, knowledge is mostly restricted to what serves his own motivation, although this now includes motivations less immediate which, when taken together, are called 'practical knowledge'. On the other hand, he usually has no more *free*, i.e. purposeless, knowledge than is engendered by curiosity and the need for diversion; yet this kind of knowledge does exist in every man, even if only to this extent. In the meantime, when motivation is quiescent, the life of man is to a large extent filled by simple *existence*, to which fact the tremendous amount of lounging about that goes on and the commonness of that kind of sociability which consists chiefly in mere togetherness, without any conversation, or at the most very scanty conversation, bear witness. Indeed, most people have – in their hearts even if not consciously – as the supreme guide and maxim of their conduct the resolve *to get by with the least possible expenditure of thought*, because to them thinking is hard and burdensome. Consequently, they think only as much as their trade or business makes absolutely necessary, and then again as much as is demanded by their various pastimes – which is what their conversation is just as much as their play; but both must be so ordered that they can be tackled with a *minimum* of thought.

Only where intellect exceeds the measure needed for living does knowledge become more or less an end in itself. It is consequently a quite abnormal event if in some man intellect deserts its natural vocation – that of serving the will by perceiving mere relations between things – in order to occupy itself purely objectively. But it is precisely this which is the origin of art, poetry and philosophy, which are therefore produced by an organ not originally intended for that purpose. For intellect is fundamentally a hard-working factory hand whom his demanding master, the will, keeps busy from morn to night. But if this hard-driven serf should once happen to do some of his work voluntarily during his free time, on his own initiative and without any object but the work itself, simply for his own satisfaction and enjoyment – then this is a genuine work of art, indeed, if pushed to an extreme, a work of genius.

Such a purely objective employment of the intellect, as well as lying behind all artistic, poetical and philosophical achievement of the higher kind, also lies behind all purely scientific achievement in general, is already present in purely scientific study and learning, likewise in any free reflection (i.e. reflection not involved with personal interest) upon any subject whatever. It is the same thing, indeed, which inspires even mere conversation if its theme is a purely objective one, i.e. is not related in any way to the interest, and consequently the will of those taking part in it. Every such purely objective employment of the intellect compares with its subjective employment – i.e. employment in regard to personal interest, however indirectly – as dancing does with walking: for, like dancing, it is the purposeless expenditure of excess energy. On the other hand, the subjective employment of intellect is, of course, the natural one, since intellect arose merely in order to serve will. It is involved not merely in work and the personal drives, but also in all conversation concerning personal affairs and material matters in general; in eating, drinking and other pleasures; in everything pertaining to earning a livelihood; and in utilitarian concerns of every sort. Most men, to be sure, are incapable of any other employment of their intellect, because with them it is merely a tool in service of their will and is entirely consumed by this service, without any remainder. It is this that makes them so arid, so brutishly earnest and incapable of objective conversation; just as the shortness of the bonds joining intellect to will is visible in their face. The impression of narrow-mindedness which often emerges from it in such a depressing fashion is, in fact, only the outward sign of the narrow limitation of their total stock of knowledge to the affairs of their own will. One can see that here there is just as much intellect as a given will requires for its ends and no more: hence the vulgarity of their aspect; and hence also the fact that their intellect subsides into inactivity the moment their will ceases to drive it. They take an *objective* interest in nothing whatever. Their attention, not to speak of their mind, is engaged by nothing that does not bear some relation, or at least some possible relation, to their own person: otherwise their interest is not aroused. They are not noticeably stimulated even by wit or humour; they hate rather everything that demands the slightest thought. Coarse buffooneries at most excite them to laughter: apart from that they are earnest brutes – and all because they are capable of only *subjective* interest. It is precisely this which makes card-playing the most appropriate amusement for them – card-playing for money: because this does not remain in the sphere of mere knowledge, as stage plays, music, conversation, etc., do, but sets in motion the *will* itself, the primary element which exists everywhere. For the rest they are, from their first breath to their last, tradesmen, life's born drudges. All their pleasures are sensuous: they have no feeling for any other kind of pleasure. Talk to them about business, but not about anything else. To be sociable with them is to be degraded. On the other hand, conversation between two people who are capable of some sort of purely *objective* employment of their intellect is a free play of intellectual energy, though the matter be never so insubstantial and amount to no more than jesting. Such a conversation is in fact like two or more dancing together: while the other sort is like marching side-by-side or one behind the other merely in order to arrive somewhere.

Now this tendency towards a free and thus abnormal employment of the intellect, together with the capacity for it, attains in the *genius* the point at which knowledge becomes the main thing, the *aim* of the whole of life; his own existence, on the other hand, declines to a subsidiary thing, a mere *means*; so that the normal relationship is completely reversed. Consequently, the genius lives on the whole more in the rest of the world, by virtue of his knowledge and comprehension of it, than in his own person. The entirely abnormal enhancement of his cognitive powers robs him of the possibility of filling up his time with mere *existence* and its aims: his mind needs to be constantly and vigorously occupied. He thus lacks that composure in traversing the broad scenes of everyday life and that easy absorption in them which is granted to ordinary men. So that genius is for the ordinary practical living appropriate to normal mental powers an ill endowment and, like every abnormality, an impediment: for with this intensifying of the intellectual powers, intuitive comprehension of the outside world achieves so great a degree of objective clarity and furnishes so much more than is requisite for serving the will that such an abundance becomes a downright hindrance to this service, inasmuch as to contemplate given phenomena in themselves and for their own sake constantly detracts from the contemplation of their connexions with the individual will and with one another and consequently disturbs and obstructs any clear comprehension of these connexions. For the service of the will an entirely superficial contemplation of things suffices, a contemplation which furnishes no more than their bearing on whatever aims we may have and whatever may be associated with these aims, and consequently consists of nothing but relationships, with the greatest possible degree of blindness towards everything else: an objective and complete comprehension of the nature of things enfeebles knowledge of this sort and throws it into disorder.

23

The difference between the genius and the normal intelligence is, to be sure, only a *quantitative* one, in so far as it is only a difference of degree: one is nonetheless tempted to regard it as a *qualitative* one when one considers how normal men, despite their individual diversity, all think along certain common lines, so that they are frequently in unanimous agreement over judgements which are, in fact, false. This goes so far that they have certain basic views which are held in all ages and continually reiterated, while the great minds of every age have, openly or secretly, opposed these views.

24

A genius is a man in whose head the *world as idea* has attained a greater degree of clarity and is present more distinctly; and since the weightiest and profoundest insight is furnished not by painstaking observation of what is separate and individual but by the intensity with which the whole is comprehended, mankind can expect from him the profoundest sort of instruction. Genius can thus also be defined as an exceptionally clear consciousness of things and therefore also of their antithesis, one's own self. Mankind looks up to one who is thus gifted for disclosures about things and about its own nature.

25

If you want to earn the gratitude of your own age you must keep in step with it. But if you do that you will produce nothing great. If you have something great in view you must address yourself to posterity: only then, to be sure, you will probably remain unknown to your contemporaries; you will be like a man compelled to spend his life on a desert island and there toiling to erect a memorial so that future seafarers shall know he once existed.

26

Talent works for money and fame: the motive which moves *genius* to productivity is, on the other hand, less easy to determine. It isn't money, for genius seldom gets any. It isn't fame: fame is too uncertain and, more closely considered, of too little worth. Nor is it strictly for its own pleasure, for the great exertion involved almost outweighs the pleasure. It is rather an instinct of a unique sort by virtue of which the individual possessed of genius is impelled to express what he has seen and felt in enduring works without being conscious of any further motivation. It takes place, by and large, with the same sort of necessity as a tree brings forth fruit, and demands of the world no more than a soil on which the individual can flourish. More closely considered, it is as if in such an individual the will to live, as the spirit of the human species, had become conscious of having, by a rare accident, attained for a brief span of time to a greater clarity of intellect, and now endeavours to acquire at any rate the results, the products of this clear thought and vision for the whole species, which is indeed also the intrinsic being of this individual, so that their light may continue to illumine the darkness and stupor of the ordinary human consciousness. It is from this that there arises that instinct which impels genius to labour in solitude to complete its work without regard for reward, applause or sympathy, but neglectful rather even of its own well-being and thinking more of posterity than of the age it lives in, which could only lead it astray. To make its work, as a sacred trust and the true fruit of its existence, the property of mankind, laying it down for a posterity better able to appreciate it: this becomes for genius a goal more important than any other, a goal for which it wears the crown of thorns that shall one day blossom into a laurel-wreath. Its striving to complete and safeguard its work is just as resolute as that of the insect to safeguard its eggs and provide for the brood it will never live to see: it deposits its eggs where it knows they will one day find life and nourishment, and dies contented.

On Aesthetics

I

The intrinsic problem of the metaphysics of the beautiful can be stated very simply: how is it possible for us to take pleasure in an object when this object has no kind of connexion with our desires?

For we all feel that pleasure in a thing can really arise only from its relation to our will or, as we like to put it, our aims; so that pleasure divorced from a stimulation of the will seems to be a contradiction. Yet it is quite obvious that the beautiful as such excites pleasure in us without having any kind of connexion with our personal aims, that is to say with our will.

My solution to this problem has been that in the beautiful we always perceive the intrinsic and primary forms of animate and inanimate nature, that is to say Plato's Ideas thereof, and that this perception stipulates the existence of its essential correlative, the *will-less subject of knowledge*, i.e. a pure intelligence without aims or intentions. Through this, when an aesthetic perception occurs the will completely vanishes from consciousness. But will is the sole source of all our troubles and sufferings. This is the origin of the feeling of pleasure which accompanies the perception of the beautiful. It therefore rests on the abolition of all possibility of suffering. – If it should be objected that the possibility of pleasure would then also be abolished, one should remember that, as I have often demonstrated, happiness, gratification, is of a *negative* nature, namely the mere cessation of suffering, pain on the other hand positive. Thus, when all desire disappears from consciousness there still remains the condition of pleasure, i.e. the absence of all pain, and in this case the absence even of the possibility of pain, in that the individual is transformed from a willing subject into a purely knowing subject, yet continues to be conscious of himself and of his actions as a knowing subject. As we know, the world as *will* is the primary (*ordine prior*) and the world as *idea* the secondary world (*ordine posterior*). The former is the world of desire and consequently that of pain and thousandfold misery. The latter, however, is in itself intrinsically painless: in addition it contains a remarkable spectacle, altogether significant or at the very least entertaining. Enjoyment of this spectacle constitutes aesthetic pleasure.

2

If, however, the individual will sets its associated power of imagination free for a while, and for once releases it entirely from the service for which it was made and exists, so that it abandons the tending of the will or of the individual person which alone is its natural theme and thus its regular occupation, and yet does not cease to be energetically active or to extend to their fullest extent its powers of perceptivity, then it will forthwith become completely *objective*, i.e. it will become a faithful mirror of objects, or more precisely the medium of the objectivization of the will appearing in this or that object, the inmost nature of which will now come forth through it the more completely the longer perception lasts, until it has been entirely exhausted. It is only thus, with the pure subject, that there arises the pure object, i.e. the complete manifestation of the will appearing in the object perceived, which is precisely the (Platonic) *Idea* of it. The perception of this, however, demands that, when contemplating an object, I really abstract its position in space and time, and thus abstract its individuality. For it is this *position*, always determined by the law of causality, which places this object in any kind of relationship to me as an individual; so that only when this position is done away with will the object become an *Idea* and I therewith a pure subject of knowledge. This is why a painting, by fixing for ever the fleeting moment and thus extricating it from time, presents not the individual but the *Idea*, the enduring element in all change. But this postulated change in subject and object requires not only that the faculty of knowledge be released from its original servitude and given over entirely to itself, but also that it should remain active to the full extent of its capacity, notwithstanding that the natural spur to its activity, the instigation of the will, is now lacking. Here is where the difficulty and thus the rarity of the thing lies; because all our thought and endeavour, all our hearing and seeing, stand by nature directly or indirectly in the service of our countless personal aims, big and small, and consequently it is the *will* which spurs on the faculty of knowledge to the fulfilment of its functions, without which instigation it immediately weakens. Moreover, knowledge activated by this instigation completely suffices for practical life, even for the various branches of science, since they direct themselves to the *relations* between things and not to their intrinsic and inner being. Wherever it is a question of knowledge of cause and effect or of grounds and consequences of any kind, that is to say in all branches of natural science and mathematics, as also in history, or with inventions, etc., the knowledge sought must be an *aim of the will*, and the more vehemently it strives for it, the sooner it will be attained. Likewise in affairs of state, in war, in finance and business, in intrigues of every sort, and so on, the *will* must first of all, through the vehemence of its desire, compel the intellect to exert all its energies so as to track down all the reasons and consequences of the affair in question. Indeed, it is astonishing how far beyond the normal measure of its energies the spur of the will can drive a given intellect in such a case.

The situation is quite different with the perception of the objective, intrinsic being of things which constitutes their (Platonic) Idea and which must lie behind every achievement in the fine arts. For the will, which in the former case promoted the endeavour and was indeed indispensable to it, must here take no part whatever: for here only that serves which the intellect achieves quite alone and by its own means and presents as a voluntary gift. For only in the condition of *pure knowledge*, where will and its aims have been completely removed from man, but with them his individuality also, can that purely objective perception arise in which the (Platonic) Ideas of things will be comprehended. But such a perception must always precede the conception, i.e. the first, intuitive knowledge which afterwards constitutes the intrinsic material and kernel, as it were the soul of an authentic work of art or poem, or indeed of a genuine philosophy. The unpremeditated, unintentional, indeed in part unconscious and instinctive element which has always been remarked in works of *genius* owes its origin to precisely the fact that primal artistic knowledge is entirely separated from and independent of will, is will-less.

3

As for the *objective* aspect of this aesthetic perception, that is to say the (Platonic) Idea, it may be described as that which we would have before us if time, the formal and subjective condition of our knowledge, were drawn away, like the glass lens from a kaleidoscope. We see, e.g., the development of bud, flower and fruit and marvel at the driving force which never wearies of producing this series again and again. Our amazement would cease if we could know that with all this changing development we have before us only the one, unchangeable Idea of the plant, which however we are incapable of perceiving as a unity of bud, flower and fruit, but are compelled to apprehend under the form of time through which the Idea is displayed to our intellect in these successive states.

4

If you consider how poetry and the plastic arts always take an *individual* for their theme and present it with the most careful exactitude in all its uniqueness, down to the most insignificant characteristics; and if you then look at the sciences, which operate by means of *concepts* each of which represents countless individuals by once and for all defining and designating what is peculiar to them as a species; – if you consider this, the practice of art is likely to seem to you paltry, petty and indeed almost childish. The nature of art, however, is such that in art one single case stands for thousands, in that what art has in view with that careful and particular deline-ation of the individual is the revelation of the *Idea* of the genus to which it belongs; so that, e.g., an occurrence, a scene from human life depicted correctly and com-pletely, that is to say with an exact delineation of the individuals involved in it, leads to a clear and profound knowledge of the Idea of humanity itself perceived from this or that aspect. For as the botanist plucks one single flower from the endless abundance of the plant world and then analyses it so as to demonstrate to us the nature of the plant in general, so the poet selects a single scene, indeed sometimes no more than a single mood or sensation, from the endless confusion of cease-lessly active human life, in order to show us what the life and nature of man is. This is why we see the greatest spirits – Shakespeare and Goethe, Raphael and Rem-brandt – not disdaining to delineate single individuals, and not even notable ones, and to make them visible before us, and doing so with the greatest exactitude and the most earnest application, in their whole particu-larity down to the very smallest details. For the par-ticular and individual can be grasped only when it is made visible – which is why I have defined poetry as the art of setting the imagination into action by means of words.

5

A work of plastic art does not show us, as actuality does, that which exists once and never again, namely the union of this particular material with this particular form which constitutes the concrete and individual; it shows us *the form* alone which, if it were presented completely and in all its aspects, would be the Idea itself. The picture therefore immediately leads us away from the individual to the pure form. The separation of form from material is already a big step towards the Idea: but every picture, whether a painting or a statue, constitutes such a separation. Now it is precisely because the aim of the aesthetic work of art is to bring us to a knowledge of the (Platonic) Idea that it is characterized by this separation, this dividing of the form from the material. It is *intrinsic* to the work of art to present the form alone, without the material, and to do so manifestly and obviously. This is really the reason waxwork figures make no aesthetic impression and are consequently not works of art (in the aesthetic sense), although when they are well made they produce a far greater illusion of reality than the best picture or statue can and if imitation of the actual were the aim of art would have to be accorded the first rank. For they seem to present not the pure form but with it the material as well, so that they bring about the illusion that the thing itself is standing there. The true work of art leads us from that which exists only once and never again, i.e. the individual, to that which exists perpetually and time and time again in innumerable manifestations, the pure form or Idea; but the waxwork figure appears to present the individual itself, that is to say that which exists only once and never again, but without that which lends value to such a fleeting existence, without life. That is why the waxwork evokes a feeling of horror: it produces the effect of a rigid corpse.

6

The reason the impressions we receive in youth are so significant, the reason why in the dawn of life everything appears to us in so ideal and transfigured a light, is that we then first become acquainted with the genus, which is still new to us, through the individual, so that every individual thing stands as a representative of its genus: we grasp therein the (Platonic) *Idea* of this genus, which is essentially what constitutes beauty.

7

The beauty and grace of the human figure united together are the will in its most clearly visible form at the highest stage of its objectivization, and this is why they are the supreme achievement of the plastic arts. On the other hand, every material thing is beautiful, consequently every animal is beautiful. If this is not evident to us in the case of certain animals it is because we are not in a position to regard them purely objectively and thus comprehend the Idea of them, but are prevented from doing so by some inescapable thought-association, usually the result of an obtrusive similarity, e.g. that of the ape to man, as a consequence of which instead of grasping the Idea of this animal we see only the caricature of a man. The similarity between the toad and mud and dirt seems to produce the same effect, although this is inadequate to explain the boundless repugnance, indeed terror and horror, which overcomes many people at the sight of this animal, as it does others in the case of the spider: this seems rather to originate in a much deeper, metaphysical and mysterious connexion.

8

Inorganic nature, provided it does not consist of water, produces a very melancholy, indeed oppressive impression upon us when it appears without anything organic. An instance is provided by the regions of bare rock without any vegetation in the long valley near Toulon through which runs the road to Marseille; but the deserts of Africa offer a much more grandiose and impressive example. The sadness of this impression produced upon us by the inorganic derives first and foremost from the fact that the inorganic mass is subject exclusively to the law of gravity, the direction of which consequently dictates everything. – On the other hand, we derive a high degree of immediate pleasure from the sight of vegetation, but this is naturally the greater the more abundant, manifold and extensive – that is to say left to itself – the vegetation is. The immediate reason for this lies in the fact that in vegetation the law of gravity seems to have been overcome, in that the plant world raises itself in precisely the opposite direction from the one dictated by this law and thus directly proclaims the phenomenon of life as a new and higher order of things.

We ourselves are part of this order: it is that in nature which is related to us, the element of our existence. Our heart is uplifted in presence of it. What pleases us first and foremost at the sight of the plant world, therefore, is this vertical upward direction, and a group of trees gains vastly from having a couple of straight-rising pointed fir-trees in its midst. On the other hand, a felled tree no longer affects us; indeed, one that has grown up slanting already produces far less effect than an upright one; and it is the down-hanging branches of the weeping willow which have surrendered to gravity that have given this tree its name. – The melancholy effect of the inorganic nature of water is in large part abolished by its great mobility, which produces an impression of life, and by its constant play with light: it is, moreover, the primal condition of our life.

9

A man who tries to live on the generosity of the Muses, I mean on his poetic gifts, seems to me somewhat to resemble a girl who lives on her charms. Both profane for base profit what ought to be the free gift of their inmost being. Both are liable to become exhausted and both usually come to a shameful end. So do not degrade your Muse to a whore.

10

Music is the true universal language which is understood everywhere, so that it is ceaselessly spoken in all countries and throughout all the centuries with great zeal and earnestness, and a significant melody which says a great deal soon makes its way round the entire earth, while one poor in meaning which says nothing straightaway fades and dies: which proves that the content of a melody is very well understandable. Yet music speaks not of things but of pure weal and woe, which are the only realities for the *will*: that is why it speaks so much to the heart, while it has nothing to say *directly* to the head and it is a misuse of it to demand that it should do so, as happens in all *pictorial* music, which is consequently once and for all objectionable, even though Haydn and Beethoven strayed into composing it: Mozart and Rossini, so far as I know, never did. For expression of the passions is one thing, depiction of things another.

II

Grand opera is not really a product of the pure artistic sense, it is rather the somewhat barbaric conception of enhancing aesthetic enjoyment by piling up the means to it, by the simultaneous production of quite disparate impressions and by strengthening the effect through augmenting the masses and forces producing it; while music, as the mightiest of the arts, is capable by itself of completely engrossing the mind receptive to it; indeed, its highest products, if they are to be properly comprehended and enjoyed, demand the undivided and undistracted attention of the entire mind, so that it may surrender to them and immerse itself in them in order to understand their incredibly intimate language. Instead of which, the mind is invaded through the eye, while listening to a highly complex piece of operatic music, by the most colourful pageantry, the most fanciful pictures and the liveliest impressions of light and colour; and at the same time it is occupied with the plot of the action. Through all this it is distracted and confused and its attention is diverted, so that it is very little receptive to the sacred, mysterious, intimate language of music. All these accompaniments are thus diametrically opposed to the attainment of the musical aim.

Strictly speaking one could call opera an unmusical invention for the benefit of unmusical minds, in as much as music first has to be smuggled in through a medium foreign to it, for instance as the accompaniment to a long drawn out, insipid love story and its poetic pap: for a spirited compact poem full of matter is of no use as an opera text, because the composition cannot be equal to such a poem.

The mass and the symphony alone provide undisturbed, fully musical enjoyment, while in opera the music is miserably involved with the vapid drama and its mock poetry and must try to bear the foreign burden laid on it as best it can. The mocking contempt with which the great Rossini sometimes handles the text is, while not exactly praiseworthy, at any rate genuinely musical.

In general, however, grand opera, by more and more deadening our musical receptivity through its three-hours duration and at the same time putting our patience to the test through the snail's pace of what is usually a very trite action, is in itself intrinsically and essentially boring; which failing can be overcome only by the excessive excellence of an individual achievement: that is why in this genre only the masterpieces are enjoyable and everything mediocre is unendurable.

12

Drama in general, as the most perfect reflection of human existence, has three modes of comprehending it. At the first and most frequently encountered stage it remains at what is merely interesting: we are involved with the characters because they pursue their own designs, which are similar to our own; the action goes forward by means of intrigue, the nature of the characters, and chance; wit and humour season the whole. – At the second stage drama becomes sentimental: pity is aroused for the hero, and through him for ourselves; the action is characterized by pathos, yet at the end it comes back to peace and contentment. – At the highest and hardest stage the *tragic* is aimed at: grievous suffering, the misery of existence is brought before us, and the final outcome is here the vanity of all human striving. We are deeply affected and the sensation of the will's turning away from life is aroused in us, either directly or as a simultaneously sounding harmony.

13

The first step is the hardest – says the popular adage. But in dramaturgy the reverse is true: the last step is the hardest. Evidence of this is the countless dramas the first half of which promises well but which then become confused, halt, waver, especially in the notorious fourth act, and finally come to a forced or unsatisfying end, or to one everybody has long since foreseen; sometimes, as with *Emilia Galotti*,* the end is even revolting and sends the audience home in a thoroughly bad mood. This difficulty of the *dénouement* is the result partly of the fact that it is easier to confuse things than to straighten them out again, but partly too of the fact that at the beginning of the play we allow the dramatist *carte blanche*, while at the end we make certain definite demands of him. We demand that the outcome shall be a completely happy or a completely tragic one – but it is not easy to make human affairs take so definite a direction. We then demand that this outcome shall be achieved naturally, fairly and in an unforced way – and yet at the same time not have been foreseen by the audience.

A *novel* will be the higher and nobler the more *inner* and less *outer* life it depicts; and this relation will accompany every grade of novel as its characteristic sign, from *Tristram Shandy* down to the crudest and most action-packed romance. *Tristram Shandy*, to be sure, has as good as no action whatever; but how very little action there is in *La Nouvelle Héloïse* and *Wilhelm Meister*!† Even *Don Quixote* has relatively little, and what there is is very trivial, amounting to no more than a series of jokes. And these four novels are the crown of the genre. Consider, further, the marvellous novels of Jean Paul and see how much inner life is set in motion on the narrowest of external foundations. Even the novels of Walter Scott have a significant preponderance of inner over outer life,

* Tragedy by Gotthold Ephraim Lessing (1729–81), a leader of the Enlightenment in Germany and the principal German dramatist before the age of Goethe and Schiller.

† *La Nouvelle Héloïse* is by Rousseau, *Wilhelm Meister* by Goethe.

and the latter appears only with a view to setting the former in motion; while in bad novels the outer action is there for its own sake. The art lies in setting the inner life into the most violent motion with the smallest possible expenditure of outer life: for it is the inner life which is the real object of our interest. – The task of the novelist is not to narrate great events but to make small ones interesting.

On Books and Writing

I

Writers can be divided into meteors, planets and fixed stars. The first produce a momentary effect: you gaze up, cry: 'Look!' – and then they vanish for ever. The second, the moving stars, endure for much longer. By virtue of their proximity they often shine more brightly than the fixed stars, which the ignorant mistake them for. But they too must soon vacate their place, they shine moreover only with a borrowed light, and their sphere of influence is limited to their own fellow travellers (their contemporaries). The third alone are unchanging, stand firm in the firmament, shine by their own light and influence all ages equally, in that their aspect does not alter when our point of view alters since they have no parallax. Unlike the others, they do not belong to one system (nation) alone: they belong to the Universe. But it is precisely because they are so high that their light usually takes so many years to reach the eyes of dwellers on earth.

2

There are above all two kinds of writer: those who write for the sake of what they have to say and those who write for the sake of writing. The former have had ideas or experiences which seem to them worth communicating;

the latter need money and that is why they write – for money. They think for the purpose of writing. You can recognize them by the fact that they spin out their ideas to the greatest possible extent, that their ideas are half-true, obscure, forced and vacillating, and that they usually prefer the twilight so as to appear what they are not, which is why their writings lack definiteness and clarity. You can soon see they are writing simply in order to cover paper: and as soon as you do see it you should throw the book down, for time is precious. – Payment and reserved copyright are at bottom the ruin of literature. Only he who writes entirely for the sake of what he has to say writes anything worth writing. It is as if there were a curse on money: every writer writes badly as soon as he starts writing for gain. The greatest works of the greatest men all belong to a time when they had to write them for nothing or for very small payment: so that here too the Spanish proverb holds good: *Honra y provecho no caben en un saco*.*

A multitude of bad writers lives exclusively on the stupid desire of the public to read nothing but what has just been printed: the journalists. Well named! In English the word means 'day-labourers'.

3

And then again, there can be said to be three kinds of author. Firstly, there are those who write without thinking. They write from memory, from reminiscence, or even directly from other people's books. This class is

---

* Honour and money don't belong in the same purse.

the most numerous. – Secondly, there are those who think while writing. They think in order to write. Very common. – Thirdly, there are those who have thought before they started writing. They write simply because they have thought. Rare.

Even among the small number of writers who actually think seriously before they start writing, there are extremely few who think about *the subject itself*: the rest merely think about *books*, about what others have said about the subject. They require, that is to say, the close and powerful stimulation of ideas produced by other people in order to think at all. These ideas are then their immediate theme, so that they remain constantly under their influence and consequently never attain to true originality. The above-mentioned minority, on the other hand, are stimulated to think by the subject itself, so that their thinking is directed immediately to this. Among them alone are to be discovered those writers who endure and become immortal.

Only he who takes what he writes directly out of his own head is worth reading.

4

A book can never be more than a reproduction of the thoughts of its author. The value of these thoughts lies either in the *material*, that is in what he has thought *upon*, or in the *form*, i.e. the way in which the material is treated, that is in *what* he has thought upon it.

The *upon what* is manifold, as are the advantages it bestows on books. All empirical material, that is everything historically or physically factual in itself and in the widest sense, belongs here. The characteristic quality lies in the *object*, so that the book can be an important one whoever its author may be.

In the case of the *what*, on the other hand, the characteristic quality lies in the *subject*. The topics treated can be such as are accessible and familiar to all men, but it is the form in which they are comprehended, the *what* of the thought, which here bestows value, and this lies in the subject. If, consequently, a book of this sort is admirable and unique, its author is so too; from which it follows that the merit of a writer who is worth reading is the greater the less it owes to his material, and even the more familiar and much-employed this material is. Thus, e.g., the three great Greek tragedians all employed the same material.

Thus when a book becomes famous you should firmly distinguish whether it is on account of its material or on account of its form.

The public is much more interested in the material than in the form. It displays this tendency in its most ridiculous shape in regard to poetic works, in that it painstakingly tracks down the real events or personal circumstances which occasioned the work, and these, indeed, become more interesting to it than the works themselves, so that it reads more *about* than *by* Goethe and studies the Faust legend more assiduously than *Faust*, And if Bürger once said: 'They will undertake learned research into who Lenore really was',* we have seen this literally come to

---

* Gottfried August Bürger (1747–94), poet. His ballad *Lenore* (1773) is one of the most famous of all German poems.

pass in the case of Goethe. – This preference for the material as against the form is as if one should ignore the form and painting of a beautiful Etruscan vase in order to carry out a chemical analysis of the pigment and clay.

5

The actual life of a thought lasts only until it reaches the point of speech: there it petrifies and is henceforth dead but indestructible, like the petrified plants and animals of prehistory. As soon as our thinking has found words it ceases to be sincere or at bottom serious. When it begins to exist for others it ceases to live in us, just as the child severs itself from its mother when it enters into its own existence.

6

Literary periodicals ought to be the dam against the ever-rising flood of bad and unprofitable books produced by the unprincipled scribbling of our age. With the incorruptibility, judiciousness and severity of their judgements, they should scourge without mercy all patchwork put together by incompetents, all the page-filling through which empty heads seek to fill their empty pockets, which is to say nine-tenths of all books, and thus work against triviality and imposture as their duty dictates; instead of which, they promote these things: and their abject tolerance allies itself with author and publisher to rob the public of its time and its money. Their writers are as a rule professors or *literati* who, because of low salaries or poor payment, write from need of money: so, since they all have a common aim, their interests are in common, they keep together, mutually sustain one another and speak in favour of one another: this is the origin of all the laudatory reviews of bad books which constitute the content of literary periodicals. Their motto ought to be: Live and let live!

Anonymity, that shield for every kind of literary scoundrelism, must disappear. The pretext for its introduction into literary periodicals was that it protected honest critics from the wrath of authors and their patrons. But for every case of this kind there are a hundred cases where it serves merely to allow complete irresponsibility to reviewers who would be unable to defend what they write, or even to conceal the shame of those so venal and abject as to recommend books to the public in exchange for a tip from their publisher. It often merely serves to cloak the obscurity, incompetence and insignificance of the reviewer. It is unbelievable what impudence these fellows are capable of, and from what degree of literary knavery they will not shrink, once they know themselves secure in the shadow of anonymity.

Rousseau already said in the preface to *La Nouvelle Héloïse*: '*Tout honnête homme doit avouer les livres qu'il publie*' – which means in English: 'Every honest man puts his name to what he writes', and universally affirmative propositions can be reversed *per contrapositionem*.* How much more this applies to polemical writings, which reviews usually are!

---

* By contraposition

7

Style is the physiognomy of the mind. It is less deceptive than that of the body. To imitate the style of another is to wear a mask, and however beautiful this may be its lifelessness soon makes it seem insipid and unendurable, so that the ugliest living face is preferable.

Stylistic affectation can be compared to pulling faces.

8

To arrive at a provisional assessment of a writer's worth it is not necessary to know *what* or *upon what* he has thought, because that would mean having to read everything he has written; it is sufficient in the first instance to know *how* he has thought. Now an exact impression of this *how* of his thinking, of its essential nature and prevailing *quality*, is provided by his style. For this reveals the *formal* nature of all a man's thoughts, which must always remain the same no matter *what* or *upon what* he thinks. It is, as it were, the paste from which he moulds all his figures, however various they may be. Just as Eulenspiegel, when asked how long it would take to reach the next town, gave his questioner the apparently senseless answer: 'Walk!' with a view to judging from his pace how far he would get in a certain time, so I read a couple of pages of an author and already know more or less how far I can profit from him.

The first rule, indeed by itself virtually a sufficient condition for good style, is *to have something to say*.

The dullness and tediousness of the writings of commonplace people might be a consequence of the fact that they are speaking only half-consciously, that is to say not really understanding the meaning of the words they use, since these are something they have learned and received finished and complete, so that what they put together is rather whole phrases (*phrases banales*) than individual words. This is the origin of the palpable lack of distinct ideas which characterize their writings, since they are without that which imposes distinctness on ideas, individual clear thinking: instead of this, we meet with an obscure indistinct welter of words, with current phrases, hackneyed expressions and fashionable locutions. Their nebulous productions consequently resemble printing with worn-out type.

With regard to the *tediousness* in writing touched on above, one should add the general observation that there are two kinds of tediousness: an objective and a subjective kind. The *objective* kind always derives from the deficiency in question, that is from the fact that the author has no clear ideas or information whatever to communicate. For he who has them goes about communicating them in a direct manner and consequently everywhere presents clear, distinct concepts, so that he is neither verbose, nor obscure, nor confused, and consequently he is not tedious. Even if his leading idea is false, it is in this event still clearly thought and well considered, that is to say at least formally correct, so that what he writes always retains some value. On the other hand, an objectively tedious work is, for the same reason, always worthless in every respect. – *Subjective* tediousness, on the contrary, is only relative: it originates in a lack of interest in the subject on the part of the reader; this, however, originates in the reader's limitations. The most admirable work, consequently, can be subjectively tedious, namely to this or that reader; as, conversely, the worst can be subjectively entertaining to this or that reader because the subject or the writer interests him.

An *affected* writer is like a man who dresses up so as not to be confused and confounded with the mob, a danger which a gentleman, however ill-clad, never runs. As a certain overdressing and *tiré à quatre épingles** thus betrays the plebeian, so an affected style betrays the commonplace mind.

Nevertheless, it is a misguided endeavour to try to write exactly as you speak. Every style of writing should rather retain a certain vestige of affinity with the lapidary style, which is indeed the ancestor of them all. This endeavour is consequently as objectionable as its converse, that is to try to speak as you write, which is at once pedantic and hard to understand.

Obscurity and vagueness of expression is always and everywhere a very bad sign: for in ninety-nine cases out of a hundred it derives from vagueness of thought, which in turn comes from an original incongruity and inconsistency in the thought itself, and thus from its falsity. If a true thought arises in a head it will immediately strive after clarity and will soon achieve it: what is clearly thought, however, easily finds the expression appropriate to it. The thoughts a man is capable of always express themselves in clear, comprehensible and unambiguous words. Those who put together difficult,

* Dressing up to the nines.

obscure, involved, ambiguous discourses do not really know what they want to say: they have no more than a vague consciousness of it which is only struggling towards a thought: often, however, they also want to conceal from themselves and others that they actually have nothing to say.

Truth is fairest naked, and the simpler its expression the profounder its influence. What declamation over the vanity of human existence, for example, can well make a greater impression than Job's: *Homo, natus de muliere, brevi vivit tempore, repletus multis miseriis, qui, tanquam flos, egreditur et conteritur, et fugit velut umbra.** – It is for just this reason that the naïve poetry of Goethe stands so incomparably higher than the rhetorical poetry of Schiller. And it is this that accounts for the powerful effect of many folk songs. Everything superfluous is prejudicial.

More than nine-tenths of all literate men and women certainly read nothing but newspapers, and consequently model their orthography, grammar and style almost exclusively on them and even, in their simplicity, regard the murdering of language which goes on in them as brevity of expression, elegant facility and ingenious innovation; indeed, young people of the unlearned professions in general regard the newspaper as an authority simply because it is something printed. For this reason, the state should, in all seriousness, take measures to ensure that the newspapers are altogether free of linguis-

---

* Job 14, 1–2: Man that is born of a woman is of few days, and full of trouble. He cometh forth like a flower, and is cut down: he fleeth also as a shadow, and continueth not.

tic errors. A censor should be instituted who, instead of receiving a salary, should receive one louis d'or for every mangled or stylistically objectionable word, error of grammar or syntax, or misemployed preposition he discovers in them, and three louis d'or for every instance of sheer impudent mockery of all style and grammar, with double the sum for any repetition, the amounts to be defrayed by the perpetrators. Or is the German language perhaps anyone's game, a trifle not worthy of that protection of the law which even a dunghill enjoys? – Miserable philistines! – What in the world is to become of the German language if every scribbler and newspaper writer is granted discretionary power to do with it whatever his caprice and folly suggest?

9

An error of style which, with literature in decline and the ancient languages neglected, is becoming more and more common, but is really at home only in Germany, is its *subjectivity*. It consists in this, that the writer is satisfied so long as he himself understands what he means: the reader may be left to make of it what he can. Unconcerned with this difficulty, the writer proceeds as if he were engaged in a monologue: while what should really be taking place is a dialogue, and indeed one in which the speaker has to express himself the more clearly in that he cannot hear the listener's questions. It is for just this reason that a style should be *not* subjective, but objective. An objective style is one in which the words are so arranged that the reader is downright compelled to think exactly the same thing as the author has thought.

But this will come about only if the author continually remembers that thoughts obey the law of gravity to this extent, that they travel much more easily from head down to paper than they do from paper up to head, so that for the latter journey they require all the assistance we can give them. If it is achieved, the words operate in a purely objective way, like a completed oil-painting; while the subjective style is hardly more effective than a series of blots on a wall: only he whose imagination has chanced to be aroused by them can see in them shapes and pictures – to others they are merely blots. The distinction in question applies to the whole mode of communication, but it can often be demonstrated in individual passages too: for example, I have just read in a new book: 'I have not written so as to increase the number of existing books.' This says the opposite of what the writer intended, and is moreover nonsense.

10

He who writes carelessly makes first and foremost the confession that he himself does not place any great value on his thoughts. For the enthusiasm which inspires the unflagging endurance necessary for discovering the clearest, most forceful and most attractive form of expressing our thoughts is begotten only by the conviction of their weightiness and truth – just as we employ silver or golden caskets only for sacred things or priceless works of art.

11

Few write as an architect builds, drawing up a plan beforehand and thinking it out down to the smallest details. Most write as they play dominoes: their sentences are linked together as dominoes are, one by one, in part deliberately, in part by chance.

12

The guiding principle in the art of composition should be that the human being can think clearly only one thought at a time, so that he should not be asked to think two, not to speak of more than two thoughts at the same time. – But this is what he is being asked to do when parentheses are inserted into sentences which have been broken up to accommodate them, a practice which causes unnecessary and wanton confusion. *German* writers are the worst offenders in this respect. That their language lends itself to it more readily than other living languages may account for the fact but does not make it commendable. The prose of no language reads so pleasantly and easily as does that of the French, and this is because it is as a rule free of this error. The French writer sets his thoughts down one after the other in the most logical and natural order possible and thus places them before his reader in succession, so that the reader can give his undivided attention to each of them. The German, on the other hand, weaves them together into an involved and twice involved and thrice involved period, because he insists on saying six things at once instead of presenting them one after the other.

The true national characteristic of the Germans is *ponderousness*:* it is evident in their gait, their activities, their language, their speech, their mode of narrating, their way of understanding and thinking, but especially in their *style of writing*, in the pleasure they take in long, ponderous, involved periods, where the memory has to bear the burden for a good five minutes, patient and unaided, until, at the end of the period, reason comes into action and the conundrum is solved. This is the kind of thing they enjoy, and if affectation and bombast can be introduced as well, the author revels in it: but Heaven help the reader.

It is obviously counter to all sound reason to clap one thought down straight over another, as if making a cross: but this is what happens when a writer interrupts what he has started to say in order to say something quite different in the middle of it, thus leaving a meaningless half-period in the custody of the reader until the other half comes along. It is like handing a guest an empty plate and leaving him to hope something will appear on it.

This form of construction reaches the height of taste-lessness when the parentheses are not even dovetailed organically into the period but, by making a straight breach in it, simply wedged in. If it is an impertinence to interrupt others, it is no less of an impertinence to interrupt oneself, as happens in a form of construction which for some years now every inferior, careless, hasty

* *Schwerfälligkeit*: heaviness, clumsiness, slowness, awkwardness, ponderousness.

scribbler with visions of payment before his eyes has employed six times on every page and enjoyed doing so. It consists – precept and example should, where possible, go together – in breaking off one phrase in order to stick another into it. They do it, however, not only from laziness, but also from stupidity, in that they take it for a pleasant *légèreté** which enlivens the discourse. – In rare individual cases it may be excusable.

13

No literary quality – persuasiveness, for instance, or richness of imagery, a talent for metaphors, boldness, astringency, conciseness, gracefulness, facility of expression, wit, striking contrast, laconism, simplicity – can be acquired by reading writers who display it. But if we already possess any such quality as a natural tendency, that is *potentia*,† we can by reading summon it up in ourselves, become conscious of it, see what can be made of it, be fortified in our inclination, indeed in the courage to employ it, judge of its effectiveness, and thus learn how to use it correctly: and only then shall we also possess it *actu*.‡ This, then, is the only way in which reading can teach writing: it instructs us in the use we can make of our own natural gifts; thus it can instruct us only when we possess such gifts. If we do not possess them we can learn from reading nothing but cold dead mannerism, and become superficial imitators.

* Lightness of touch.   † Potential   ‡ In fact.

14

As the strata of the earth preserve in succession the living creatures of past epochs, so the shelves of libraries preserve in succession the errors of the past and their expositions, which like the former were very lively and made a great commotion in their own age but now stand petrified and stiff in a place where only the literary palaeontologist regards them.

15

According to Herodotus, Xerxes wept at the sight of his enormous army to think that, of all these men, not one would be alive in a hundred years' time; so who cannot but weep at the sight of the thick fair catalogue to think that, of all these books, not one will be alive in ten years' time.

16

The art of *not* reading is a very important one. It consists in not taking an interest in whatever may be engaging the attention of the general public at any particular time. When some political or ecclesiastical pamphlet, or novel, or poem is making a great commotion, you should remember that he who writes for fools always finds a large public. – A precondition for reading good books is not reading bad ones: for life is short.

17

Buying books would be a good thing if one could also buy the time to read them in: but as a rule the purchase of books is mistaken for the appropriation of their contents.

18

In the history of the world half a century is a considerable period, because its material is always changing, inasmuch as something is always happening. In the history of literature, on the other hand, half a century is often no time at all, because nothing has happened: things are as they were fifty years before.

It is consistent with this state of things that we should see the scientific, literary and artistic *Zeitgeist* declared bankrupt about every thirty years: for during this period the errors contained in it have grown to such proportions as to crush it by the weight of their absurdity, while the opposing view has at the same time been strengthened by them. So now there is a sudden change: but what often succeeds is an error in the opposite direction. To exhibit the periodical recurrence of this state of things would be the true pragmatic material of literary history.

I wish someone would one day attempt a *tragic history of literature*, showing how the various nations which now take their highest pride in the great writers and artists they can show treated them while they were alive. In such a history, the author would bring visibly before us that endless struggle which the good and genuine of all ages and all lands has to endure against the always dominant bad and wrong-headed; depict the martyrdom of almost every genuine enlightener of mankind, almost every great master of every art; show us how, with a few exceptions, they lived tormented lives in poverty and wretchedness, without recognition, without sympathy, without disciples, while fame, honour and riches went to the unworthy; how, that is, their lot was that of Esau, who while out hunting and catching game for his father was robbed by Jacob of his father's blessing; but how, in spite of all, love of their cause sustained them, until the hard struggle of such an educator of the human race was at last consummated, the never-fading laurel-wreath beckoned and the hour struck in which for him too:

> *Der schwere Panzer wird zum Flügelkleide,*
> *Kurz ist der Schmerz, unendlich ist die Freude.**

---

* The heavy armour becomes the light dress of childhood; the pain is brief, the joy unending.